ASTROLOGY MADE EASY

'ASTARTE'

Published by
Melvin Powers
WILSHIRE BOOK COMPANY
12015 Sherman Road
No. Hollywood, California 91605
Telephone: (213) 875-1711 / 983-1105

CONTENTS

First published and
Copyright © 1967
by Bancroft & Co.
(Publishers) Ltd.
Greencoat House, Francis Street,
London SW 1
Printed in the United States of America

ISBN 0-87980-009-7

THIS little book is intended as a *practical* intro-
duction to the art and science of Astrology. Remem-
bering the difficulties which confronted me when I
was first grappling with its intricacies, I shall try
to explain everything in the simplest possible way,
and I will leave out all but the essential astronomical details, which usually form an unnecessarily
large, and tedious part of any textbook on it. Likewise, other than in the list of recommended biblio-
graphy which will be appended, I shall not refer
to the very numerous writers of renown from
whose works various details of technique have
been added to Ptolemy's fundamental principles.

Much that is in this book is based upon my own
personal experience as a professional of thirty years
persistent astrological work, experience gleaned
from contact with thousands of clients whose charts
are in my files. I can therefore vouch for such information as concerns the zodiacal types, the effects
of planetary groupings and also for the validity of
the System of House Division employed in the calculation of horoscopes, a system which has recently
come under much attack, largely from misguided
astrologers who are poor exponents of their craft.

The whole basis of Astrology rests upon the
assumption that human character and fate can be
understood by linking both with the activity of our
Solar System. Astrology is purely and simply a
method of correlating that which is born or
begun with the positions of the Sun, Moon and
planets in the Zodiac at the time this happens.
Using these as symbols of phenomena, attributes and
potentialities, and drawing upon the evidence provi-

ded by past experience, the astrologer makes his deductions.

The awkward situation for those critics who dismiss Astrology as unscientific hocus-pocus is that it works, and works to a sufficiently consistent and persistent degree to exclude any element of pure chance. Its methods are not always fool-proof, but where they fail the reason seems to be imperfect understanding and faulty interpretation, and, again, the difficulty at times of being certain of the time-factor involved, rather than to falsity in the theory.

If you are prepared to take the trouble to learn the fundamentals of astrological technique you should be able to arrive at a much clearer understanding of yourself and the people around you, and also to handle your affairs on a much better basis. If you have the least ingredient of imagination in your make-up you will be led into fascinating speculation. If you lack spiritual faith, the emphasis that Astrology places upon the belief in some Prime Intelligence directing Man to a higher purpose may help to restore this.

In order to understand and practise Astrology you will have to acquire a little astronomical knowledge (which will be a painless process, I assure you); and you will be using simple mathematical calculations well within the skill of anyone who can do simple sums of addition and subtraction. You will have to exercise your memory quite a lot, for your must store up certain details; but this will not be tiresome as they are so very fascinating in themselves.

And what rich rewards you will have for your trouble! If for no other reason than that it is always stimulating to take up a new hobby, and the more so if it can be a useful one.

2: FUNDAMENTALS: TYPES

ASTROLOGY divides humanity by twelve, four and three. There are twelve different zodiacal archetypes, drawn from four groups corresponding to the Elements of Nature, Fire, Earth, Air and Water, themselves divided into another triad called Qualities. The Qualities describe the functions of the Elements.

But there are also other divisions. One is that by which the twelve archetypes become masculine or feminine. This does not have any strictly sexual implication for, obviously, any type includes people of both sexes; more correctly, it corresponds to those who are predominantly Extravert or Intravert, Active or Passive in temperament.

The other division is into the "Planetary" types; properly this should not include Sun and Moon types, as the former is a luminary and the latter a satellite; but for the sake of convenience they are put under this heading.

In this chapter I shall deal with the Elements, Qualities and Planetary types, and give a detailed description of the zodiacal archetypes, which embody all three, in the next chapter.

The underlying idea behind all this system of division and subdivision is that, though there are, broadly speaking, twelve distinctly different kinds of people, some share basic features in common, others are in conflict, whilst there are also those which have little impact on each other. None are totally isolated from, or immune to the rest.

THE ELEMENTS

Fire

Collectively, the three members of the Fire group are distinguished by abundant physical vitality; they are dynamic, idealistic, and their self-assertiveness and self-assurance are expressed by a desire to excel or dominate; emotionally they are ardent, quickly aroused, sociable. These are the pioneers, leaders and organisers of Society.

Their characters are reflected in their physique, which gives a hint of the tremendous force within them; they look healthy, have a good muscular development, resonant voices; and their movements are flexible.

These people are linked with the zodiac signs Aries, Leo and Sagittarius; and their birthdates are as follows: (*)

> ARIES – March 21st/April 20th
> LEO – July 22nd/August 21st
> SAGITTARIUS – November 22nd/
> December 20th

Earth

The common denominator of the three Earth types is their stability of character. They are Ma-

(*) The human types are named after the *Constellations* of the Zodiac. At the time when Greek Astrology linked the two together, there was only one Zodiac; but nowadays there are two. The second is the Mathematical Zodiac, a system of time-measurement of the Sun's apparent journey through the heavens; and the birthdates listed are those which accord with the "Signs" (time-divisions) of the Mathematical Zodiac. (The significance of the two Zodiacs will be fully explained in a later chapter.) The birthdates are approximate ones; the Sun's movement being slightly irregular makes it impossible to categorically determine the exact time it will enter or leave any sign each year. It does so, normally, around the 20th/23rd days of each month, except in February, when it does so around the 19th. People born at the close of the third week or beginning of the fourth week of any month are a blend of two signs and are called "Cuspal" types.

terialists, and are sensible, shrewd, cautious, conservative, consistent and tenacious. Their emotions are less easily aroused but are more sustained. They are not creative, but they perpetuate, safeguard and make more useful the things initiated by the Fire types. They come under the heading of Administrators.

Physically they are usually well built, with a large bone-structure, but seem coarser, and are not so magnetically attractive as the Fire people. They have quieter voices, their bearing is less imposing, and they are much slower in movement, firmer in their tread.

The Earth types are linked with the signs Taurus, Virgo and Capricorn; and their birthdates are as follows:

TAURUS – April 21st/May 20th

VIRGO – August 22nd/September 21st

CAPRICORN–December 21st/January 19th

Air

The three Air types have a much more delicate, refined air about them than the first two. Finely etched features of a more aquiline cut, and a particularly intelligent look mark them out in any crowd. In fact, intelligence is the mainspring of their characters, and their emotions are filtered by it. They are versatile, adaptable and fundamentally restless in spirit, and their bias is towards idealism rather than a materialistic outlook. They are the most cultured of the four main elemental types.

Physically, they are agile, light of movement; their speech is fluid and fairly rapid; their voices light in tone.

Air people come under the dominion of the signs Gemini, Libra and Aquarius; their birthdates are

as follows:—

GEMINI – May 21st/June 20th

LIBRA – September 22nd/October 22nd

AQUARIUS – January 20th/February 18th

Water

This group of three comprises the most highly sensitive, impressionable, receptive and malleable people. They are guided by their instinct, and they are acutely intuitive, very imaginative. Because their emotions are so active, they find it difficult to be objective in their attitude. They can be highly creative, particularly in the Arts. They are also innately humane. They incline more to idealism than materialism, but can be swayed by sensual urges.

The Water types tend to be more rounded in figure than the others. The skin of all three tends to be more opaque, and it can be rather pallid. Their eyes are particularly expressive, but not so much of intelligence as of emotion. Because the trunk of the body is rather large, their limbs seem to be disproportionately short. They have a gliding, or rolling gait. Their manner varies from one of reserve to shyness; but this will change according to the company they keep.

The Water types come under the signs Cancer, Scorpio and Pisces; their birthdates are as follows:

CANCER – June 21st/ July 21st

SCORPIO – October 23rt/November 21st

PISCES – February 19th/March 20th

The relation between Fire and Air is usually good because Fire needs oxygen to burn, and Air is warmed by Fire.

But Fire does not blend well with Earth or

Water. Whereas Air assists Fire to extend itself and Fire produces the warmth which keeps air in circulation, if earth is heaped on fire it will reduce it to smouldering, and water thrown upon fire will quench it. Conversely, Fire can reduce earth to ashes and it evaporates water.

Earth and Water help each other; banked by earth, Water finds a causeway for itself to effect its progress. Earth needs to be moistened by water to prevent it cracking and disintegrating. Earth can be scattered by Air; and when Air is confined by earth it becomes stale, lifeless. Air and Water can be mutually dissipative; and too much Air will freeze moisture, destroying itself in the process.

Fire/Air are Active, Earth/Water Passive.

The qualities

It is very difficult to give a simple explanation of the Qualities. I have yet to come across a textbook on Astrology which clearly defines this subtle definition of types. Even their names do little to help; it sounds bizarre to call them Cardinal, Fixed and Mutable (or Common) in view of some of the attributes of the signs of the zodiac to which they correspond.

The three Quality groups are most easily understood if we think of them as defining three different types of behaviour, behaviour which reflects. the basic nature of the three Elements Fire, Earth and Air. They are therefore related to what is created, preserved, diffused or communicated and the manner in which this is done.

Cardinal quality types

The cardinal people are those born under Aries (Fire) Cancer (Water) Libra (Air) and Capricorn

(Earth). In their own ways they all create something by their projective energy.

Aries creates action by pitting itself against the world at large in a desire for conquest. Cancer creates a nucleus of security within the limits of its immediate environment because of its desire for refuge. Libra desires to enlarge its scope without disturbing the balance of things, and by pooling its energy creates harmony with everyone and everything around it. Capricorn endeavors to create permanence but may only produce stagnation.

These aims are striven for by the means provided through their Elemental sources. Aries through its fiery impetuosity, enthusiasm; Cancer through a fluid propensity to nourish what surrounds it; Libra through its airy flexibility; Capricorn through its earthy tenacity, its rigidity.

Fixed quality types

Preservation is the common aim in the behaviour of Taurus, Leo, Scorpio and Aquarius people. They are united by their fixity of purpose, their single-mindedness, their aversion to any unnecessary change.

As Taurus is the Earth sign of the group, its preservative instinct is purely materialistic; it becomes acquisitive of possessions. Leo is affected by its generative instinct, and turns its fiery vitality into inspiring and organising other people.

Scorpio, the Water type, attempts to conserve emotion. It becomes the victim of itself and can be a danger to others by its storing up of its emotional force when this is carried to extreme limits. It can be a self-disciplined sign by reason of its own strength, its endurance; but when, like Taurus. it

turns acquisitive kills the object of its emotional desires. It must learn to share in order to conserve.

Aquarius, the Air type, is selective; slowly, persistently it sifts what it considers to be most valuable, worthy of preservation, rejects the rest, and then regenerates what it has kept and by this means multiplies – and distributes – its bounty. Like Leo, it organises – but on a bigger scale. It knows that if anything is to endure, it must also be transmitted, not hoarded.

The Mutable (Common) types

People born under Gemini, Virgo, Sagittarius and Pisces all belong to this group; theirs are "dual" signs; and duality is their common characteristic. By their behaviour they introduce variety, contrasts; to do so they must work, not alone, but through the other groups.

They are restless, volatile, vacillatory in the ways in which they act.

Gemini, the Air type, is mentally explorative; garners much information which it then relays indiscriminately. Virgo, the Earth type, is practical, industrious and seeks to perfect its own and the efforts of others. Sagittarius, the Fire type, is creative and behaves in a way intended to liberate itself and others. And Pisces, the Water sign, allows its duality, its fluidity an emotional outlet – it merely seeks union with all and sundry. It wishes to experience all, and to share all experience.

We have now run the gamut of all the major types. Read them over again and again until you have thoroughly memorised and understood them, for they hold the key to all astrological interpretation. They can only serve as a general framework for all the possible mutations of human nature and human activity, so complex, so devious at times; but you will gain more and more insight into character by pondering over them.

The planetary types

These merely form a repetition of the types we have already run through. The linking of a planet with any one of the zodiac signs will give you a quick summary of its characteristics.

When Ptolemy laid down the rules for modern Astrology, astronomers knew of only five planets: Mercury, Venus, Mars Jupiter and Saturn. They had to apportion these and the luminaries among twelve signs of the zodiac; so each of the five planets is assigned to two zodiac types. There is a very important distinction here; for when linked with one type it will express what is most favourable to itself, and in the other it will signify the distortion of its attributes. It is in harmony with one sign, but in an inharmonious relationship with the other.

THE "SUN" TYPE.

Assigned to LEO (July 22nd/August 21st)

Physically:

has a large, round head, bold, prominent eyes (usually light in colour); smooth, warm skin which reacts quickly to exposure; fine, silky hair, receding at the temples, and growing back from the head in a mane; deep chest, body narrowing at the flanks. Handsome rather than beautiful. Has a dignified manner; sophisticated air; and a resonant voice. Carries the head high. Cat-like tread.

Characteristics:

Sociable, but demands respect. Autocratic but benevolent; independent, generous, loyal, proud and idealistic. An instinctive leader. Loves luxury, appreciates beauty; craves power. Affection, companionship, sympathy and flattery are essential to the Sun type. They are romantic, and possessive. Jealousy, exaggerated self-esteem, complacency, periodic laziness, extravagance are faults. Stable nervous system; very strong constitution.

THE "MOON" TYPE.

Assigned to CANCER (June 21st/July 21st)
Physically:

Round face, pale, smooth, elastic skin; light-coloured, often green, eyes (one larger than the other); retroussé nose; plump body, small, podgy hands, feet,

Left Mrs Jacqueline Kennedy (Sun) *Camera Press;* *above* Charles Laughton (Moon) *Karsh*

broad nails, short limbs. Lank, thin hair; the women are very full-breasted. Nautical or crablike walk; dreamy expression, diffident manner, soft thin voice lisps. Leisurely in movement.

Characteristics;

Sensuous, imaginative, psychic; emotional and very impressionable, imaginative; sympathetic, kindhearted. Strong family-attachment (particularly towards the mother, probably resembles her). Highly domesticated, but loves change, travel. The "Moon" type can be very moody (reacting to the lunar phases); they quickly take offence, are stubborn, untidy, inclined to procrastinate. The women are easily moved to tears and use them as a very skilful weapon. Emotional life follows a vivid but unstable course. Health governed largely by emotions.

THE "MERCURY" TYPE.

Assigned to GEMINI (May 21st/June 20th) and VIRGO (August 22nd/September 21st)

Physically:

Slim and of average height; small bones, large and usually dark eyes which are very brilliant; sharply pointed, long nose which twitches or reddens in moments of emotion; deeply indented lines between nose and upper lip; long slim hands, fingers, feet. A great many wear spectacles. Very mobile features, mannerisms. High—pitched voice; very quick speech. Incessantly restless.

Below Maurice Chevalier (Mercury) *Camera Press; right* Brigitte Bardot (Venus) *Black Star*

Characteristics:
Inquisitive, loquacious; eager for knowledge; the studious type. Adaptable, versatile; lively wit; quick to learn. Lack concentration, continuity, decisiveness; very prone to criticise and gossip. Live on their nerves. Flirtatious, friendly, but not passionate. Personal relationships are very numerous, but casual and short-lived. Best in subordinate positions, as responsibility frightens them. Wiry constitution; never put on much weight.

THE "VENUS" TYPE.
Assigned to TAURUS (April 21st/May 20th)
and LIBRA (September 22nd/October 22nd)
Physically:
Pretty, often very beautiful, if a woman; slightly effeminate, if a man. Large, glistening, gentle eyes;

Above Marlon Brando (Mars) *Tom Smith;*
right Walt Disney (Jupiter) *Karsh;*
far right Dr Albert Schweitzer (Saturn) *Peter Bruchmann/ Quick*

usually blue. Small mouths, short upper lip and full underlip; small, even teeth; oval face, regular features; wavy or curly hair. Both sexes have sloping shoulders, small hands and feet; are lissom in youth, but put on weight later. Dimples in cheeks, chin, limbs. Birdlike way of holding head on one side whilst talking or listening; amiable weakness for preening themselves before mirrors, windows – anything that throws back their reflections. Symmetrical bodies. Melodious voice.

Characteristics:

Tolerant; diplomatic; peace-loving, placid. Artistic; put comfort and pleasure before everything. Lack driving force, but marvellous opportunists. Flair for acting as go—betweens. Very good bargainers. Laziness, lack of firmness, instinct for compromise and vanity are faults; and they can be selfish. Throat, kidneys are vulnerable bodily parts.

THE "MARS" TYPE.
Assigned to ARIES (March 21st/April 20th)
and SCORPIO (October 23rd/November 21st)
Physically:

Aquiline profile; strong facial lines; prominent facial bones; upper portion of head recedes sharply; bone-ridge over eyes very prominent. Ruddy complexion;

strong, large white teeth; men delight in moustaches or beards; women have a faint down on the upper lip; both have profuse bodily hair. Muscular, sinewy, lithe; crisp hair on head; varies through all the shades of red to jet black. Scar, birthmark, mole on head or face. Clumsy movements. Piercing gaze; resonant voice; may be harsh. Defensive or belligerent manner.

Characteristics:

Frank, forceful, courageous, adventurous, impulsive; good powers of leadership, organisation, but lack of attention to detail, patience, tolerance. Explosive temper; inclined to be physically violent. Sports-mad; mechanically-minded; prone to accidents. Ambitious; extravagant; like change, travel; the outdoor life; may be devoid of artistic feelings. Passionate; sensual; jealous to the highest degree. High rate of vitality, but nervous system sensitive. When ill, have an exceptionally high temperature.

THE "JUPITER" TYPE.

Assigned to SAGITTARIUS (November 22nd/December 20th) and PISCES (February 19th/March 20th).

Physically:

Plump in youth, even plumper from middle age. Round head, high forehead, large, prominent eyes, which slant slightly at the corners; honey-coloured or purplish complexion; small ears, bones; long limbs; slim hands, feet. Voice rather "plummy"; very jovial manner. Benign demeanour; slightly pompous as they grow older; leisurely gait.

Characteristics:

Just, humane, conventional and conservative. Generous; love pomp and ritual; inclined to be snobbish and, sometimes, hypocritical. Self-indulgent. Sociable; interested in Religion, Philosophy; fondness for associating themselves with clubs, societies. Ambitions; always do things on the grand scale. "Lucky". The Micawber type. Constitution good; but suffer from a sluggish liver; boils.

THE "SATURN" TYPE.
Assigned to CAPRICORN (December 21st/ January 19th).

Physically:
Small head, deepset eyes, aquiline features; prominent nose, ears, which have some very distinctive pe-

culiarity; poor teeth; strong lines crease the forehead and face; lantern-jawed in later life. Expression very serious, sad. Large strong frame, with very prominent bone structure, joints; ungainly hands, feet. Thin, lifeless hair. Walk with head bent. Slow movements; slow speech; toneless voice; flat-footed.

Characteristics:

Conservative; cautious; methodical; taciturn; very reliable; logical; practical but unimaginative. Very obstinate; creatures of habit. Shrewd in assessing people, weights, measures, values. Retentive memory. Unsentimental; but deeply faithful; strong sense of duty. Faults are being too dogmatic; inflexibility; over-serious outlook; lack of humour. Very fond of, often talented at Music. Dress in drab colours. Very thrifty; self—sacrificing for those they love. Seem to be destined to have a hard life, heavy responsibilities, many frustrations, delays; but do extremely well from sixty onwards and live a very long time. Prefer solitude to company. Martyrs to rheumatoid complaints.

Apart from these traditional types, three others have been been added by the discovery of Uranus, Neptune and Pluto. They are linked with Aquarius, Pisces and Scorpio.

THE "URANUS" TYPE.

Assigned (together with the traditional "Saturn" type) to AQUARIUS (January 20th/February 18th).

Physically:

Long face; broad forehead, jowl, but narrow or receding chin; crisp curling hair, often radiating out over the head. Large eyes which glow with a living fire — their most arresting feature. Arched brows; patrician features; slim, long limbs; beautiful filbert

Above Charles Dickens (Uranus)
right Frederic Chopin (Neptune) *Radio Times Hulton Picture Library*

nails. Magnetic appearance and personality; staccato, disjointed but highly graphic way of talking; curiously disjointed, or mechanical movements. Body assymetrical.

Characteristics:

Restless, original in thought, speech, action, habits; erratic, perverse; apt to do the blankly unexpected at times of crisis. Idealistic, intellectual, creative and always quick to thumb their nose at authority, convention. Wayward; fanatically enthusiastic, but inconsistent. Very independent; detached; yet good organisers and are very humane in disposition. Moody; but always courteous. Incapable of recognising their mistakes. Inspirational. Have sensational life-history; suffer estrangement from friends, relatives; ardently erotic and coldly celibate by turns. Hyper-sensitive nervous system; often suffer from eye-trouble or circulatory disorders.

THE "NEPTUNE" TYPE.

Assigned to PISCES (jointly with the traditional "Jupiter" type): February 19th/March 20th.

Physically:

Round face, large, gentle eyes; ethereal expression or an absent-minded appearance. Forehead marked

with fine lines; Delicate features; very fleshy cheeks; long lashes; sensitive hands. The women have the type of looks which the painter Rosetti depicted; the men have theatrical good looks. Manner is dreamy; voice soft, with a slight stammer; speech slow. Silky hair is another physical distinction; the men go prematurely bald.

Characteristics:

Charming but untidy; like way-out clothes and a very free and easy way of life. Present styles of teenagers very typically Neptunian. May not be too fussy about washing. Inspirational; intuitional; artistic; intensely sensitive. Very musical; dramatically talented. Illogical, elusive and escapists by instinct; not always truthful; highly emotional; extremely sentimental; secretive; forgetful. Very careless about money-matters; not ambitious; often very unwordly.

The life-history of the Neptunian is strange and chaotic.

THE "PLUTO" TYPE.

Assigned to SCORPIO (with the traditional Mars type) October 23rd/November 21st.

Very little can be written about this type, as research goes back only to the time of the discovery of the planet in 1930. Any conjecturing on the effects of Pluto, other than those which can be demonstrated by evidence gained since 1930 must therefore be highly speculative. But, if Pluto is very prominent in a horoscope it is certainly likely to bring about a very profound change not only in personality but in the actual fundamental character of the person at some time in life. Moreover, this could also very radically affect the physical appearance.

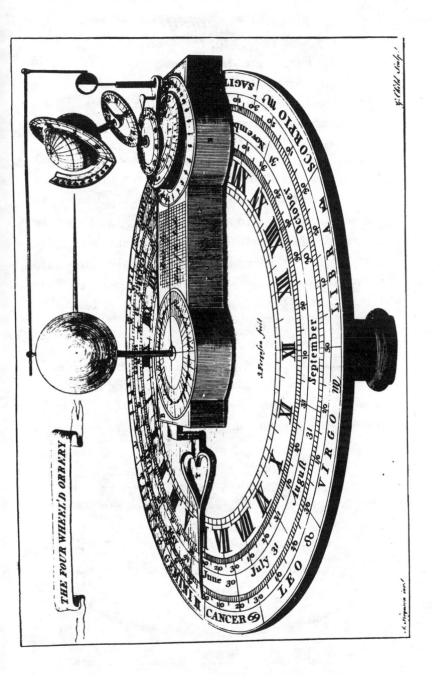

THE FOUR WHEEL'D ORRERY

J. Ferguson fecit.

SCORPIO · LIBRA · VIRGO · LEO · CANCER · GEMINI · SAGITTARIUS

November · October · September · August · July 31 · June 30

3: THE ZODIAC TYPES

The Ram, the Bull, the Heavenly Twins
And next the Crab, the Lion Shines,
The Virgin and the Scales,
The Scorpion, Archer and Sea Goat,
The Man who held the Watering Pot
And Fishes with glittering tails.

Isaac Watts; hymn-writer and composer
of doggerel verse. (1674–1748.)

THE names and symbols of the twelve constellations of the Zodiac date back to the times when men expressed their ideas in picture-writing, and so they are convenient reminders of the characteristics associated with different types of people. They also show how closely the old astrologers observed their fellow human beings, and how accurately they pinpointed their idiosyncrasies.

Of course it would be quite easy to rename the zodiacal types to fit in with the scientific classications used in Medicine, Psychology and Pathology today. But it seems a pity to deprive them of their picturesque associations for no better reason than a

preference for clinical terminology. After all, the Zodiac deals with all the aspects of Man and his activities, and neither he nor they can be adequately described in scientific ways.

The descriptions which follow will give you a comprehensive dossier of each type, according to its Element, Quality, planetary ruler and active or passive nature.

But bear one important thing in mind. You are never going to meet up with anyone who exactly corresponds to his or her "sun-type" for it would be astronomically impossible to find the Sun, Moon and all the planets gathered together in any one sign at any moment in time. Everyone is a mixture of solar, lunar and planetary ingredients coloured by their background of sign-positions and grouped together at the time of birth; you will have to learn to be very perceptive, very discriminative, in making any judgment about other people—and about yourself, too. But you will have one thing to help you: all the people born under any one sign will have, at the core of their being, certain qualities in common with each other which distinguish them from others born under different signs.

ALL ABOUT ARIES—"THE RAM"

Classification: 1st sign of the Zodiac, through which the Sun appears to move between, approximately, March 21st and April 20th of any year. People born then are Sun-in-Aries individuals.

Symbol: ♈.

Element: Fire.
Quality: Cardinal.
Nature: Positive, hot and dry.
Planetary ruler and its symbol: Mars (♂).

Appearance:

Height: Average.

Type of Body: muscular, sinewy, strong, large-boned. Long trunk, straight back, jutting pelvis.

Head: long, and of medium breadth, central part of back of head emphasised. The head is wide at the top, but narrow at chin, which is wedged, often has a cleft. Hair: this type is hairy; hairgrowth is crisp, curled or wavy, and on the head it grows upward and backward, forming into horns above the temples. The colour is often red.

Forehead: high and wide, with a pronounced bone-ridge above the eyes, making them seem deepset. Bushy eyebrows.

Face: cheek-bones prominent; nose long, aquiline; wide mouth, with thick, highly-coloured lips. Ears are large and have long lobes. There are lines on the face (vertical one above eyes, lines running from nose to corners of mouth). The head is thrust forward over the neck, which is long.

Shoulders: sloping.

Skin: coarse, open-pored; reddish tinge to complexion.

Teeth: large and strong.

Hands: powerful, but lacking refinement in shape.
Facial expression: stern. Colour of eyes varies, but is more often dark and the gaze is very penetrating.
Voice and way of speaking: loud, unmusical tone; brusque in manner.

Movements: rapid, conveying impression of tremendous energy, but clumsy.

Comments on Appearance: Aries men have a special fondness for moustaches or beards; both sexes dislike headwear.

This type is fashion conscious, look their best in casual country clothes or sports-wear, and both sexes look handsome in uniform. Handsome is a more apt description than beautiful for the women, who have a slightly masculine look. Aries hates

Actor and writer Peter Ustinov: Sun in Aries
R. Gordon Wilson

tight-fitting clothes; its taste is a little loud. Both sexes are quick to adopt new fashions. The men favour ornate tie-pins, signet rings, wrist-watches; the women prefer large pieces of jewellery, very strong scents.

Mannerisms:

Mania for opening windows, doors, when they have to be in enclosed surroundings. But, when cross, apt to slam doors and break objects, if they cannot otherwise physically assault the object of their displeasure.

Character:

Uncomplicated. Very forceful, ego-centric, combative. Arians are single-minded, adventurous, enterprising but are apt go to the extreme in all behaviour. So they can be wilful, reckless, ruthless, rude. They are both idealistic and very ambitious; but they are not tolerant, patient or sympathetic, for they despise weakness. This type can be sadistic when angry, but its anger fades quickly, and then it does not bear a grudge.

Mentality:

Aries has an inspirational, imaginative mind but is not able to think very deeply, and its sense of humour is crude.

Emotions:

Very strong, and the most dominant force in the nature, in fact. Aries is passionate, can be very loyal whilst its affection lasts, has a very powerful sex-urge; but is interested only in conquest, and lacks affectionate qualities.

Failings:

These can be summed up by saying that they all stem from lack of self-control, and they include vanity, selfishness, jealousy, lustfulness. By instinct, Arians are inclined to be honest, but when in the grip of ambition can be unscrupulous. However, they are never subtle, so it is easy for other people to outwit them.

Relationships:
Very stormy, whether they be with the family, friends, working associates or marriage-partner. Aries is not capable of a give-and-take attitude in personal dealings with other people.

Affinities:
The other two Fire signs, Leo and Sagittarius.

Antipathies:
Watery Cancer and Earthy Capricorn. The result of association with its opposite sign, Libra, will depend on whether the Libran is of the same, or the opposite sex. Aries and Libra can get on if of opposite sexes, but not otherwise.

Best occupations:
Those which are challenging, demand much physical strength or energy, and which have an adventurous aspect to them. Such as: the Defence Services; politics; higher echelons of the Civil Service; anything to do with mechanism, such as engineering; and anything to do with tools, weapons or pyrotechnics. Arians make good surgeons, butchers, farmers (for they love an outdoor life) professional sportsmen; animal-trainers or animal-hunters.

In Commerce Aries will be attracted to company promoting, and be specially interested in the constructional industries.

Both sexes are unflagging careerists who aim for

the highest peak of achievement; neither is daunted by failure, and usually overcomes it more than once in life. But failure is usually of their own making rather than due to unfortunate circumstances. Both prefer independent status or positions of authority; neither can tolerate a subordinate role.

Handling of money:
Aries only wants money for what it can buy; spends it very lavishly; likes to gamble in a big way, is very prompt in paying debts and willing to loan cash.

Physical Constitution and Health:
Arians have strong constitutions, but are susceptible to feverish ailments from which they recuperate very quickly. Actually, they are more prone to accidents than illness; and if they have not a birthmark on the head or face they will have a scar there. This sign of the zodiac rules the head and to some extent the brain, so that illnesses may affect the latter.

The Life-Pattern of Aries:
Will be full of action from start to finish. As a rule, the 27th, 36th and 63rd years are especially important ones.

The following are traditionally linked with Aries; the No. 9; the colour Scarlet; Tuesday; Iron; the Ruby.

Cuspal Types: these are people born in the first five and last five days of the Aries period; they will be less typical than the rest, having, respectively, something of Pisces or Taurus in their make-up.

ALL ABOUT TAURUS—"THE BULL"

Classification: 2nd sign of the Zodiac, through which the Sun appears to move between approximately, April 21st and May 20th of any year.

Symbol: ♉

Element: Earth.

Quality: Fixed.

Nature: Negative (or Passive), cold, dry.

Planetary ruler and its Symbol: Venus (♀)

Appearance:

Height: Taureans are of medium height, or below average height, but very seldom tall.

Type of Body: thickset, square, with a large trunk and short limbs. The limbs are rounded, but very slim in comparison to the body, and the feet are particularly dainty.

Head: medium long and also round in shape, with the central part of the back slightly bulging. The chin is rounded, often dimpled; dimples are also evident in cheeks, hands, knees, elbows. Hair: thick, soft but strong in growth, very often curly. There is a forelock in the centre of the forehead similar to the bull's tuft. The hair is more often dark than light, usually brown.

Forehead: prominent and round, also low, and strongly developed in lower portion.

Face: also round. This is a fleshy type, and this is specially noticeable in the cheeks and around the jowl. The nose is short, quite large, with very distended nostrils; the mouth wide, but with well-shaped, cupid's bow, full and slightly pouting lips. Ears are soft and round, especially at the lobes. Eyebrows are curved. The neck is very short, thick and full-throated. Women have the "girdles of Venus".

Shoulders: broad, but rounded; and this type is heavy-chested, the women having especially large breasts.

Skin: creamy in colour, soft and opaque in texture.

Teeth: small and even.

Hands: large, fleshy with soft palms, but well shaped, and the fingers taper at the ends.

Facial Expression: placid-in fact, slightly bovine. The eyes are the most beautiful features, being large, heavy-lidded, prominent, but ingenuous in their gaze; the whites of the eyes are very lustrous.

Voice: very musical (this is the sign of the singer). The manner of speaking is friendly, rather slow.

Movements: Taureans take short steps. In spite of its weight and of appearance of strength, this type is very light on its feet and a graceful dancer.

Comments on Appearance; there is something sensual in the looks of the Taurean. In the crudest types this can also become grossness.

Taureans are very interested in clothes, and have quite good taste; but they want them to be comfortable as well as attractive. Both sexes are rather conservative in taste, buy of the best but make their garments last, and both like jewellery and scent.

Mannerisms: two unconscious traits which betray the bovine signature. When irritated, the women tap their feet, and the men move their heads slowly from side to side; this is the signal that the Bull is about to charge.

Popular English singer Marianne Faithfull: Sun in Taurus

Character:
Taurus is a materialistic type and very pragmatic. Caution, conservatism, tenacity, practicality and patience are the outstanding qualities.

Mentality:
Taurus is a slow thinker and rather limited in mental outlook and interests. Opinions, once formed, are seldom changed; so they become prejudices. This is a type which has a robust sense of humour, is slow to anger, but once aroused, takes a long time to forgive and forget. Because of the association of Venus with this sign, many Taureans are artistically talented, and the majority appreciate beauty and the Arts—especially Music.

Emotions:
Very deep, and very stable, but Taurus is not

emotionally exuberant. When in love, the Taurean displays a very sentimental streak; and, where the affections are involved, Taurus can be very generous. The sex-urge is strong; but though this type likes to flirt, it is very loyal when in love.

Failings:

Those which stem from lack of flexibility and a too down-to-earth outlook. Obstinacy, acquisitiveness, jealousy, fits of laziness, vanity, greediness (including over-eating—Taurus has a gluttonous streak); lack of enterprise. Hide-bound habits.

Relationships:

Are usually peaceful as a whole. Taureans are attached to their families and to their friends, but friends come from within a small circle which does not extend beyond the family or working connections.

Romance plays a powerful part in the Taurean's life before marriage; but once married, he or she settles down; this type is not very prone to divorce. Marriage is usual in the middle twenties. Taureans are domesticated to the extent of being dependant on home-comforts, but Mrs. Taurus is not enthusiastic about household duties. Being very sociable in spirit, they do a lot of home-entertaining but also like to go to the gay spots for amusement. Taureans are indulgent parents.

Affinities:

The two Earth types, Virgo and Capricorn.

Antipathies:

Fiery Leo and Airy Aquarius. Taurus blends especially well with its opposite number, Scorpio, in marriage-partnership; but when of the same sex, Taurus and Scorpio are implacable foes.

Best occupations:

All those which can be regarded as being very "safe"; which involve a consistent routine and are not too demanding, mentally. Also all those which can be guaranteed to produce very ample incomes, as this is the sign which is very money-conscious. Professionally, many accountants, bankers, economists and stockbrokers come from this group; but Taureans also link up with architecture and everything else connected with building, land and property. Many enter the Arts or the entertainment world; others go into the luxury trades and industries. A few become doctors, but never surgeons (Taurus has no skill with edged tools). Lower down in the social scale, you will find pawnbrokers, second-hand dealers, publicans.

The special flair of Taurus is its administrative skill; it can work easily in a subordinate position, and extremely well in partnership.

Handling of money:

Taurus has tremendous financial acumen; and makes money work for itself. This type intends to be able to retire in comfort at sixty. But Taurus does not stint on personal expenditure.

Physical Constitution and Health:

Taurus is very strong, and is blessed with a very stable nervous system. But if deeply upset, emotionally, this will acutely affect the health. However, illness is rare, but when ill recuperation is slow. This sign of the zodiac rules the ears, nose, throat, thyroid gland and tonsils. Taurus hates unnecessary exercise, but needs a lot, as it puts on weight easily.

The Life-Pattern of Taurus:

Will be one of slow but steady progress.

The 24th and 42nd years are usually especially important ones.

The following are traditionally linked with Taurus: the number 6, blue-green shades of colour; Friday; the Turquoise; Copper.

Cuspal-types:

These are the people born in the first five and last five days of the Taurus period; they will be less typical than the rest, having, respectively, something of Aries or Gemini in their make-up.

ALL ABOUT GEMINI—"THE TWINS"

Classification: 3rd sign of the Zodiac, through which the Sun appears to move between, approximately, May 21st and June 20th of any year. People born then are Sun-in-Gemini individuals.

Symbol: Ⅱ

Element: Air.

Quality: Mutable (or Common).

Nature: Positive or Active, hot and moist.

Planetary ruler and its Symbol: Mercury (☿).

Appearance

Height: usually above average, very seldom below.

Type of Body: very slim, with a short trunk and long limbs. This type can look rather frail.

Head: is long in shape, and narrow between the ears; but above this the shape is slightly bulging on each side.

Hair: this is fine and straight, becomes sparse as time goes by. It is often light in colour. This type does not, as a rule, possess much bodily hair.

Forehead: this is very "brainy"; broad, high and well developed but also slightly receding towards the top, which emphasises the development of the lower central part. Eyebrows are thin, almost straight.

Face: the features are finely etched, aquiline, and facial bones are easily visible; the nose is thin, long, pointed, and it has a very inquisitive look; nose-twitching is frequent in this type. Sometimes the tip is slightly bent. The mouth is thin, but wide; the upper lip protrudes; the indentation between the upper lip and centre of the nose is very pronounced. Size of eyes vary, but the expression is always very alert, and sometimes the eyes are very bright. They are usually wide-set.

The ears are well shaped, and stand out a little.

Shoulders: Gemini has broad shoulders which are very square.

Skin: this is very fine, with the veins showing clearly through. The complexion tends to be pale.

Teeth: the teeth are not too strong; calcium content is below normal in many Geminians.

Hands: long, slim; the fingers are large-jointed; this type is often ambidexterous, or double-jointed.

Facial expression: very lively, very mobile.

Voice and way of speaking: the voice is light, sometimes shrill; but this is also the sign of the born mimic. Speech is very rapid; the Geminian continually interrupts others whilst in conversation with them, as their thougths race ahead.

Movements: extremely quick. restless, nervous. Geminians run rather than walk. This type cannot relax.

Comments on Appearance: this is one of the types which is usually wearing spectacles, as minor defects of vision are common.

Geminians are able to wear youthful clothes indefinitely, as there is something of the Peter Pan about them. Gemini likes "separates", two-piece combinations; and has a weakness for too many accessories. The Gemini man is always plentifully supplied with pens, pencils, and a clutter of objects in his pockets; the women have overloaded handbags, and always carry some letters around with them in these.

American singer and film actress Judy Garland: Sun in Gemini *Jerry Watson*

Mannerisms:

Gesticulation, for one thing. Fidgetting with objects; lack of attentivness.

Character:

This is the first of the "dual" signs, as its name suggests; so Geminians are two-sided in character. Adaptability, versatility, and a love of novelty are three outstanding traits. There is a very powerful urge to communicate. But this is not a type which has any real strength of character, or much stamina; in an emergency they go to pieces completely.

Mentality:

It is intellect which governs Gemini; but the intelligence of Gemini is superficial rather than profound. These people can learn anything very rapidly, but are too easily diverted from one interest to another. However, there is certainly capacity for creative thought; very good powers of self-expression in speech and writing, and Gemini has a wonderful sense of humour which is typically American in type; slack, subtle. Cockney wit is also typical of Gemini.

Emotions:

Very much on the surface. Gemini is friendly but cannot be deeply touched. The sex-urge is not strong; this is a type which is perfectly happy in platonic relationships with the opposite sex.

Failings:

Diffusiveness; inaccuracy (Gemini is full of information, but don't rely too much on what he tells you); gossip; sheer nosiness; lying (Gemini will prevaricate easily in order to extricate himself from embarrassment); too much preoccupation with trivial details; untidiness.

Relationships:

Those within the family are the most important, as Gemini is much attached to relatives and very much involved in their lives. Socially, this type makes a tremendous amount of acquaintances, but few deep friendships; even when it has close friends it fails to keep them, as it is a case of "out of sight, out of mind." And as a Gemini moves from place to place fairly frequently, contact is soon lost.

Romance is seldom very ardent, but Gemini does tend to marry early; and may marry twice.

Mercury, the ruling planet of the sign, is the symbol of youth; and Geminians are wonderful at handling children, due to their own childlike traits. But this is not a very fertile sign.

Affinities:

The other two of the Air Group, Libra and Aquarius.

Antipathies:

Earthy Virgo and Watery Pisces. Link-ups with their opposite type, Sagittarius, can be very unsettling, as the exuberant qualities of "The Archer" leads poor Gemini out of its depth.

Best Occupations:

Those which are focussed on brainwork—any kind of brainwork. And those which are connected with travel, transport. Such as: education; journalism/literature; Public Relations; courierwork; salesmanship (Gemini has a glib tongue); entertainment. All kinds of clerical activities.

Geminians much prefer to work with or for others than to go it alone. They are apt to change jobs, even careers, rapidly; sometimes follow two different occupations at the same time.

Handling of money:

Gemini does not have any difficulty in making money, but hardly ever ends up with a fortune. They spend easily, have no stamina for tough bargaining. The truth is, they do not care enough about money to concentrate on earning a great deal.

Physical Constitution and Health:

Gemini has a wiry constitution, but lives on its nerves, and it is these which are the cause of most of its illnesses. This type is a very light sleeper, often a sleepwalker. Gemini is connected with the lungs, and also with the arms and shoulders. It is most important for Gemini to have plenty of fresh air, and a regular regime as regards eating and sleeping, in order to maintain good health.

The Life-Pattern of Gemini:

Very changeful, but does not go to extremes; actually, it is the twenties which may be the period of greatest opportunity; for Gemini is often spectacularly successful then—only to burn itself out at thirty, whereafter it seems to drift.

The following are traditionally linked with Gemini: the number 5, Wednesday; pale yellow or neutral shades such as faun; Quicksilver; the Topaz.

Cuspal types:

These are the people born in the first five and last five days of the Gemini period; they will be less typical, having, respectively, something of Taurus or Cancer in their make-up.

ALL ABOUT CANCER—"THE CRAB"

Classification: 4th sign of the Zodiac, through which the Sun appears to move bet-

ween, approximately, June 21st and July 21st of any year. People born then are Sun-in-Cancer individuals.
Symbol: ♋
Element: Water.
Quality: Cardinal
Nature: Negative, Cold and moist.
Ruler of the sign and its Symbol: The Moon (☽).

Appearance:

Height: most Cancer people are rather short, and very few are above average height.

Type of Body: large trunk, short limbs. Plump in build. But this is after early youth; at first, many Cancerians are slim, but with rounded limbs. This type has weak joints.

Head: egg-shaped; very wide between the ears; and the chin is rounded; the head is quite high above the forehead.

Hair: of medium strength and quality; usually straight. This type does not have much bodily hair.

Forehead: of average size, rounded and slightly prominent just above the nose.

Face: round. The features can be quite delicate in youth, but tend to coarsen later. Cheeks are rounded; the mouth is full; the nose tiptilted or saddle-shaped; the lips are well shaped. Cancer eye-brows seemed to be raised questioningly. The ears are odd, as they tend to be angular — and large.

Eyes: rather prominent often very light — or green in colour; can be dewy, or watery. (Cancer is often afflicted with weak eyes). Sometimes the eyes are assymetrical.

The neck is short, wide, the throat rounded.

Shoulders: medium width, rounded. The women born under this sign are large-breasted.

Skin: pale, very opaque; this is a very fleshy type, and in later years the features seem to lose their shape because of this. The skin can also become very flaccid, as the muscular system is weak.

Teeth; poor in quality.

Hands; very plump, with short fingers, broad at the tips.

Facial expression: rather gentle as a rule, but can also seem very suspicious. Again, there is sometimes a faintly somnolent look about the eyes, over which the lids drop. The face of Cancer changes with its moods, which alternative rapidly. So this type can look dreamy, "moony", placid; but it seldom looks really animated.

Voice and way of speaking: the tone is low, and the speech slow, often hesitant; sentences are left unended, or there are long pauses between speech. But, when emotionally stirred, there is a particularly sympathetic, beguiling way of speaking.

Movements: Cancer either rolls along nautically, or sidles along like its namesake, the Crab.

Comments on appearance: I have described the most usual type of Cancer; but there is another: taller, with very pinched features and a fretful expression; in this type, the eyes are small, beady, and the manner extremely reserved.

Cancer does not really care much about fashion, and, being economical, spends little on dress; but as women of this type are good with their needle, they fashion attractive garments for themselves. It's an odd thing, but clothes soon look shabby on Cancer; they become crumpled, limp (compare with Pisces).

Queen Juliana of the Netherlands:
Sun in Cancer *Camera Press*

Miss and Mrs. Cancer, the most feminine of women, were never intended by Nature to wear slacks, sports-clothes; but look wonderful in décolleté evening gowns.

Mannerisms:

Very crablike indeed. Just as the crustacean encircles its claws around an object, Cancerians instinctively clasp their tummies when in repose. When idle, the fingers of their hands also curl inwards, and they tuck their thumbs into their palms.

They delight in giving their companions a playful nip, but they can tweak, verbally, when provoked, and this is very painful for the recipient!

Character:

Cancer is an introvert type. Timidity, sensitivity, an overwhelming urge for security in conflict with a restless desire for experience make the Cancerian very temperamental. But all born under this sign are fundamentally cautious, prudent, untiringly persistent for what they most desire; and they are very practical.

Mentality:

The mind of Cancer operates through the emotions, and this gives keen insight, very acute intuition. It also gives a vivid imagination—but no instinct to be logical. Many Cancer people are artistically inclined, this being, in particular, the Painter's and Poet's sign. The sense of humour is rather gentle; the memory remarkably good.

Emotions:

Very deep, very assimilative. The emotional attitude is sentimental and protective; very romantic. Being exceptionally receptive to external sensations, laughter and tears come very readily to Cancer. But tears are more frequent, for there is often a slightly melancholy strain. Even when deliriously happy, the instinct is to burst into tears. Men born under this sign have a feminine (not effeminate) streak, and can really understand how women feel.

Failings:

Lack of initiative; vacillation; instinct to put things off; sulkiness; stubbornness; instinct to hoard; meanness; imitativeness. Suspiciousness; overdue reticence.

Relationships:

Cancer is related to the home, motherhood, and all aspects of domesticity. The family means everything to the Cancer-born, and their life is centred around it. So friends will be those shared with relatives; the partner will be one approved of by the family. Marriage usually occurs around 28th year of age; but may do so around the 21st year if the Cancer person lacks a home-life, relatives. After marriage, the instinct is to rear a family.

Affinities:

The two other Water types, Scorpio and Pisces.

Antipathies:

Fiery Aries and Airy Libra. Though Cancer and Capricorn do often mate together, it is doubtful whether the union is satisfactory, as their natures are so very much directly opposite.

Best Occupations:

Those, which deal with basic needs, especially domestic needs. Anything connected with farming, catering, building. Also the humane professions, and in particular obstetrics or nursing. Municipal work. Among the Sciences, those of physics, biology, chemistry.

Cancer and the Moon have to do with the Sea, with fluids, so the Marine Services, aquatic activities, and anything to do with the licensed trades, too, attract this type.

Cancer women prefer marriage and motherhood to any other career, and they are the forces behind many successful men.

Another interesting thing about Cancer is its propensity for carrying on a family business or profession. The Cancer person can exercise authority, but is not ambitious for personal distinction and thus is not ambitions for personal distinction and thus is quite happy in an unobtrusive position, so long as it is a safe one.

Handling of money:

This is an extremely economical sign; and it can become a miserly one. Occasionally, Cancer will gamble, but only when it has a really strong hunch about the result.

Physical Constitution and Health:

Cancer people are healthy, but their systems are as absorbent as sponges. Yet, oddly enough, they can be healthy when living in low-lying, damp areas, but this is because of their watery link-up. They are very sensitive to changes of weather—and to changes of the Moon, too! This sign links up with the chest, breasts, stomach, uterus, the alimentary system and the ductless glands. There is very often a slight defect in sight. But Cancer is one of the longest-living of the zodiac types, for it takes great care of itself, and grows healthier as it grows older.

The Life-Pattern of Cancer:

Travel figures prominently, at some time or other, in the Cancer; but eventually this type will return to its homeland. There is a very definite seven-year cycle pattern and the 28th and 49th years are outstandingly significant.

The following are traditionally linked with Cancer: the Numbers 2 and 7; Monday; the colour white; the Pearl or Moonstone and Silver.

Cuspal Types; these are the people born in the first five and last five days of the Cancer period; they will be less typical because they have something of Gemini or Leo in their make-up.

ALL ABOUT LEO—"THE LION"

Classification: 5th sign of the Zodiac, through which the Sun appears to move between, approximately, July 22nd and August 21st any year.

People born then are Sun-in-Leo individuals.

Symbol: ♌

Element: Fire.

Quality: Fixed.

Nature: Positive, Active, hot and dry.

Ruler of the sign and its symbol: The Sun (☉).

Appearance:

Height: most Leos are of average height, but some are much taller.

Type of Body; this is very strong, with a full trunk, but proportionate limbs; and the whole body is well made. Leo rules the spine, among other things, and there is often a slight spinal weakness, or curvature. As though conscious of this, Leo carries itself with the head held high, seeming to lean back very slightly in order to correct the irregularity.

Head: large, sometimes disproportionately so, and round, but at front and sides, flat at the back; something very distinctive about this particular shape of head.

Hair: rather fine in texture, wavy or curly and usually light rather than dark in colour; grows back from the brow like the lion's mane; it recedes early in life. The hair of Leo shines like an aureole around the head.

Forehead: round, wide and medium height.

American film actress Lucille Ball: Sun in Leo

Face: Well formed nose, large nostrils, rather thin, firm mouth, the lower lip slightly protuding; strong jaw and chin. But curiously enough, the chin sometimes seems weak, receding. Closer inspection will however prove this wrong. Leo has rather fine eyebrows, slightly rounded; large, long ears, and the lobes grow into the side of the head (women born under this sign must have the ears pierced if they are to be able to wear ear-rings comfortably).
The eyes are very striking; large, wide open, vibrant with life.

Shoulders: broad, but slightly drooping. This type is full chested, but the women have surprisingly small bosoms for their build.

Skin: the texture is very good, the colour very healthy. The Leo skin is exceptionally sensitive, and peels or browns in sunlight very quickly.

Teeth: unfortunately, the teeth are not usually very strong or particularly attractive.

Hands: very capable, well made but large, palms very large and warm to the touch. The Leo body is always warm to touch.

Facial expression: commanding, but very frank in look. Something of the sun is to be seen in the Leo look, which magnetically attracts attention, respect.

Voice and way of speaking: voice is full-toned, speech decisive, commanding. It ascends to a roar when the lion is angry.

Movements: very energetic; Leo has a dignified carriage, and, in movement, is catlike—light, slightly sinuous.

Comments on Appearance: not only does the Leo type impress others with its dignity, moving like a lion among the community; but vitality seems to flow from this type.

Leos love clothes and any other kind of adornments; are most happy if circumstances permit them to wear regalia of any kind, always have an overstocked wardrobe, are always in the fashion. But, alas, the taste is a little loud; they overdo everything. In particular, there is a fondness for furs, jewellery and vivid colours. Of course, everything they wear or own is of the best, for they cannot tolerate the second-rate.

Mannerisms:

Very catlike. They knead cushions, stroke materials like velvet sensuously, pass their tongue across their lips with satisfaction, eat daintily like the domestic pussy; and they spit or scratch (metaphorically) when annoyed.

Character:

Pride lies at the root of the Leo character. Ambition, self-assurance, complacency, very good organising ability, tenacity, conservatism and a natural instinct for leadership are all Leo traits. Loyalty is perhaps the greatest of all.

Mentality:

This appears to be greater than it is; for the Leo confidence is such that others over-estimate their intelligence. There is an inspirational flair on occasion, but the greatest mental asset of Leo ·is the ability to marshal ideas together. Opinions are firmly held. Sense of humour is not too highly developed, and Leo cannot see a joke against itself. But a good many Leos have artistic talent.

Emotions:

Very powerful, very sustained; possibly the most warm-hearted type of the zodiac. To give and receive affection, to have companionship, are vitally important to the wellbeing of Leo, and this type wilts in solitude. Dissillusionment over the affections can be a deeply searing experience to Leo, who is naturally idealistic and romantic in spirit.

Failings:

Vanity; gullibility; laziness; extravagance (no Leos ever live within their income); excessive pride; arrogance; and a too domineering attitude. Excessive conservatism is a great handicap at times.

Relationships:

Vitally important element in the Leo life-history. Leo is proud of and loyal to its family; very faithful in friendship and in love; but alas attracts too many parasitic friends. The Leo popularity is great because Leos are over-generous; underlying it there is much jealousy in the attitude of those they befriend.

Affinities: the other two Fire signs, Aries and Sagittarius.

Antipathies:

Earthy Taurus, Watery Scorpio and Airy Aquarius. Very seldom indeed does Leo, even when of opposite sex, come to terms with its opposite, Aquarius. They do on occasion exhibit a very powerful mutual attraction, but it does not last long.

In romantic and marital life, Leo is very possessive, but extremely devoted. Marriage, alas is seldom completely a success; somehow the Leo manages (probably because of its gullibility) to link up with a partner who does not fulfil all its needs. But unhappily married Leos will not willingly divorce; instead, they get involved in triangular situations which drag indefinitely. Marriage is most usual around the 30th year.

They love home, but do not want to be bothered with the tedious side of household life; as soon as possible, Leos will employ servants to run the menage. The Leo family is small, but almost invariably includes a son; and Leo parents rather overwhelm their children in their efforts to do their best for them.

Best occupations:

The professions, for a start; Leo is really more suited to these than Commerce. The Church, the Law, Medicine and the academic world are suitable for Leo. But it is an exhibitionist sign, with strongly dramatic instincts, and is completely at home in the entertainment world. Leos are naturally attracted to any occupation that has some glamour, some dignity about it.

If they go in for business, then the choice will be towards the luxury trades and industries.

Leo, of course, naturally gravitates to the top of its profession or business; not so much through hard work, or talent, but self-confidence carries it there. And, sooner or later, Leos will be directing other people. Partnerships are dubious, for the Leo is too dominant. There is only one thing Leo has to guard against in order to maintain its success; and that is the instinct to neglect work for pleasure, or to become too complacent.

Handling of money:

Very careless. Leos spend prodigally; but they are usually lucky with money, too. Leos are dilatory about paying bills, not because of dishonesty, but because they can't be bothered to write out the cheques. They should get their banks to deal with their regular commitments in order to avoid being dunned by creditors.

Physical Constitution and Health:

Leo has a very strong constitution, and looks as healthy as it feels. Its stamina is almost inexhaustible. And it has a very stable nervous system. Leo has a most stimulating effect on those who are ill, who draw strength from it. This sign of the zodiac rules the heart and the dorsal region of the spine; and in later life various heart-irregularities may develop.

The Life-Pattern of Leo:

This is stable, and usually follows ten-year cycles; the forties and sixties are the peak periods.

.The following are traditionally linked with Leo: the Number 1, all shades of yellow, orange (colours of sunlight); Sunday; Gold; the Diamond; Amber.

Cuspal Types: these are the people born in the first five and last five days of the Leo period; they will be less typical because they have something of Cancer or Virgo in their make-up.

ALL ABOUT VIRGO—"THE VIRGIN"

Classification: 6th sign of the Zodiac, through which the Sun appears to move between, approximately, August 22nd and September 21st of any year. People born then are Sun-in-Virgo individuals.

Symbol: ♍

Element: Earth.

Quality: Mutable.

Nature: Passive, cold, dry.

Planetary ruler and its symbol: Mercury (☿).

Appearance:

Height: medium to below average. The tallest are those born at the beginning of the period.

Type of Body: this can be quite delicate, or it can be more compact. The limbs are longer than the trunk in all types. Joints are solid.

Head: Virgo has a round, short head, but it is well proportioned.

Hair: poor in quality and rather sparse in growth, indiscriminate in colour. Little bodily hair.

Forehead: one of the best features; it is high, rather flat, but wide; very fine lines are soon etched on it, but they do not age the face. Eyebrows are fine and beautifully shaped.

Face: Virgo has good features. Because the face is quite full, the features seem to be dug into it. The nose is the least attractive feature, as it is rather coarse at the end, though aquiline in shape. The mouth is sensitive, but with a short upper lip which makes the lower one seem fuller and more protruding. The size of the mouth is small. Ears are round, with large lobes. Virgos have sturdy necks, rather short.

Shoulders: these are broad, square.

Skin: pale, but good in texture.

Teeth: of average size; quite strong.

Hands: large, but though capable, also look refined; fingers taper, nails are well-shaped.

Facial expression: varies. There is an intelligent, often anxious look; but some types have a particularly gentle, rather sad expression in the eyes. The eyes of Virgo are very intelligent, can be very large and beautiful.

Voice and way of speaking: the voice of Virgo is disappointing. It can sound very flat, it is normally quiet, but becomes shrill when there is tension. Virgo speaks pedantically, and is full of small talk.

Movements: easy, quick but tread slightly heavy.

Comments on Appearance: it is the neatness, the cleanness of the Virgo which strikes the eye. There is something of the fussy bachelor, the prim old maid, even about those who try to be very debonair or sophisticated.

Virgo always dresses unobtrusively, but in excellent taste; the effect is dull. Both sexes are, like Gemini, rather youthful looking, and at their best when in very simple clothes. Both seem to have a special fondness for fine tweeds. Neither cares much for jewellery. Miss and Mrs. Virgo use make-up very prudently, prefer light, clean-smelling perfumes.

Mannerisms:
Very like those of Gemini; fidgetty–Gemini,

British film actor and comedian Peter Sellers:
Sun in Virgo *Camera Press*

too, they are gesticulative, though rather less mobile in features.

Character:

Practical by nature, there is something essentially reliable about the Virgo character. Virgo people have a very strong sense of duty, of probity; they tend to be rather inhibited and are very conventional by instinct. They are particularly good at executive work.

Mentality:

Virgo is a predominantly intellectual, and a completely rational type. Very reflective, highly analytical, introspective and a mental perfectionist, obsessed by details. Memory is retentive, and for this reason this type has an encyclopaedic mind; but they lack originality. They are intended to be the critics, not the creators. Very often there is no sense of humour at all; but there can be a caustic wit.

Emotions:

Subordinated to the mind; the emotional attitude is cool, kind, never ardent. Relationships with other people are conditioned by the sense of duty rather than by strong magnetism.

Failings:

First and foremost, lack of self-confidence and an inbuilt anxiety complex. Hair-splitting; fussiness; small-mindedness; the instinct to nag. A too submissive, humble attitude, and an over serious, pessimistic outlook on life.

Relationships:

Unexciting but enduring. Even when not in harmony with relatives, Virgo will remain dutiful towards them, and often sacrifices itself needlessly for the family. Friends are selected because of an intellectual attraction, or because the Virgoan is accustomed to their company through working proximity or family connections. This type does like to link itself with cultural or humane groups, and willingly takes on the more tedious chores in connection with these.

Affinities:
The two other Earth types, Taurus and Capricorn.

Antipathies:
Airy Gemini, Watery Pisces—the opposite sign to Virgo. Close association between these two, in marriage or in any other way, is usually mutually disastrous. With Fiery Sagittarius, poor Virgo is completely out of its depth, mentally, emotionally and even physically; for the exuberance of this sign exhausts the Virgoan.

Virgo matures late, and romance is not usually a prominent feature of the life much before thirty; it is after thirty that Virgo wakes up to the fact that it is missing something important. This type has no strong sex urge, but the instinct to do as others do, the fear that abstention may affect health, sanity leads the Virgoan into tepid adventures.

But much depends upon the partner Virgo chooses; if they mate with a full-blooded, warmhearted type husband or wife it can perform wonders for Virgo, which has an adaptable streak in its make-up.

However, it is certainly true that a lot of Virgoans seek marriage-guidance, find their way into the psychologist's or psychiatrist's consulting rooms; for Virgo really enjoys discussing sex or any other problems ad infinitum.

Both sexes are domesticated, and insist on a well-run home; are very conscientious parents.

Best Occupations:
Those of an intellectual character, and anything to do with the welfare of their community. Any kind of work which involves classifying, tabulation. The professions which most suit this type are dentistry, education, accountancy, literary or journalist work of an editorial nature; all kinds of laboratory work; domestic science. Quite a few become psychologists or psychiatrists, but the lack of emotional insight can handicap their work.

Unassuming and unambitious, Virgo is perfectly content to be a member of the hive; thrives in the Civil Service, in large organisations, companies; and is not fitted for an independent, or heavily responsible position, because of its nervous disposition.

Handling of money:
Virgo is very, very frugal; never gets into debt; and is over cautious, so it loses opportunities to make a fortune. But Virgo always ends up with reasonable financial reserves.

Physical Constitution and Health:
Of all the zodiac types, Virgo is the one which is most preoccupied with health and hygiene. Though many people born under this sign don't look particularly robust, they are in fact very wiry and live to a very ripe old age. Partly because they take such care of themselves, and become food-faddists, keep-fit fanatics. How they love to discuss ailments, operations; and, no matter how limited their imagination in other directions, it is most fertile in creating illusions about personal ailments. Ill health becomes an escape for the Virgoan in difficulties.

Virgoans have the best-stocked medicine cabinets of anyone, and are a boon to the manufacturers of patent medicines. Give them an attractive little pill-box for a birthday or Christmas present, and you will keep them happy.

This sign is connected with the digestive processes, the intestines, the gall-bladder and the appendix, (Most Virgoans acquire an appendix scar, for they seem determined to get rid of this appendage).

The Life-Pattern of Virgo:
Rather prosaic, but exemplary. Progress starts in career from around the 25th or 30th year, and is maintained thereafter. Virgo never retires; if one job comes to an end at sixty, the Virgoan will busy itself on something new. For this type cannot be idle.

The following are traditionally linked with Virgo; the Number 5, soft neutral shades of grey, fawn, mushroom, or the duller shades of yellow (mustard); Wednesday; the Topaz; Quicksilver.

Cuspal Types: these are the people born in the first five and last five days of the Virgo period; they will be less typical as they have something of Leo or Libra in their make-up.

NOTE: All that I have written about Virgo makes them seem rather drab characters. Don't be misled, however: these are the people who make the cogs of life go round much more smoothly for their fellows. They are essentially good in character, and should never let themselves be diverted from their natural instincts because of criticisms or ridicule. All they need to do is to cultivate more self-esteem, a little more selfishness, and learn to enjoy life.

ALL ABOUT LIBRA—"THE BALANCE"

Classification: 7th sign of the Zodiac, through which the Sun appears to move between, approximately, September 22nd and October 22nd of any year. People born then are Sun-in-Libra individuals.

Symbol: ♎

Element: Air.

Quality: Cardinal.

Nature: Positive, hot, moist.

Planetary ruler and its Symbol:

Venus (♀)

Appearance:

Height: This varies a good deal, according to the period of birth; Librans born in September are shorter as a rule than those born in October, and those born in the second week and up to the middle of the third week in October are sually well above average height.

Type of Body: well-proportioned as regards trunk and limbs. But the ankles and feet may mar an otherwise very attractive appearance; the former are thick, the latter surprisingly plump, with short toes. Again, Librans born in the 2nd/3rd weeks of October have better-shaped ankles and feet.

Head: this is round at the top, but rather long, narrowing towards the chin (often dimpled, as are the cheeks). The head falls away very perceptibly at the back from the crown.

Hair: fine in texture, silky in appearance; even if brown, tends to be light rather than dark in colour. Very little bodily hair.

Forehead: medium in height, very full, rounded in shape (this type seldom wrinkles). Delicately traced eyebrows, curved.

Face: oval in shape; the features being very good indeed, and very delicate, the mouth is small, sensitive, and opens to reveal small, even, shining teeth. Librans often have the classical Greek shape of nose. Pretty ears. The neck is slim, supple, of medium length.

Shoulders: a give-away in the men, as they are usually narrow and slightly drooping. But Librans born around October 3/12 have high, square, broad shoulders.

Skin: very fine and delicate in youth; becomes blotchy, mottled, with broken veins apparent, later.

Hands: oval, with long, delicate fingers, tapering at tips.

Facial expression: very amiable, and much enhanced by the beauty of the eyes, which are large, dewy, expressive. A particularly high proportion of blue, or hazel-eyed people are born under this sign.

Voice and way of speaking: very gentle, melodious tone of voice; easy, unhurried but alert way of talking.

Movements: very graceful—there is perfect poise.

Comments on Appearance: this is the sign of symmetry, and Librans are the exception who have symmetrical features and proportions among the zodiac types. But there is a look of weakness of character about this type.

Grooming is perfect; Librans are very conscious of their appearance. This is the sign of good taste, of moderation in all things, including fashion. But the men do sometimes seem a little effeminate in their addiction to discreet jewellery, silken or very finely textured underwear, hairstyles. (Incidentally there is an instinct in both sexes to adopt a central hair-parting).

Mannerisms:
Usually there is an aversion to smoking. Notice the way, when weighing up any statement or proposition the Libran will carefully balance some small object, such as a pencil, on the tip of a finger, or balance himself on his toes.

Character:
The traditional descriptions of the Libran are apt to be rather too complimentary. True, in the best specimens there is a very equable disposition, a love of justice, and an idealistic outlook. But some very discontented, peevish and far from estimable individuals are born under this sign. The basic ingredient in the psychological make-up of Libra is the urge for harmony, the desire to balance opposites. This makes for much discrimination; but it also means that in him or herself the average Libran is usually in a state of mental and emotional flux. Librans are extremely adaptable, versatile, artistically inclined; wonderful as intermediaries.

Mentality:
This is a highly imaginative, intelligent type, but memory is poor. Also the instinct for balance, though it makes for an analytical attitude of mind, does not make for profundity, as this would mean carrying thought-processes to the ultimate point. Skilful in discussion, the Libran is equally skilful in evasion. A diplomatist, par excellence.

Emotions:

Like the mental faculties, these tend to be superficial rather than deep. They are not sustained; but the emotional adaptability is such that Librans can get on well with all around them. They have a give-and-take attitude, but manage to get the best of any such exchange.

Failings:

Those which stem from the very qualities which are more desirable — i. e., the peace-loving, adaptable instincts. These make for too great a capacity for compromise; for vacillation, evasion. There is a too calculating attitude about the Libran. In the more primitive specimens, this makes for some very undesirable traits — artfulness, selfishness. Though physically not aggressive, the Libran will find an outlet for discontent or grievances by stirring up trouble for others, just as successfully as they can bring about peace for them.

Relationships:

This type is completely dependent on others for any kind of stimulus, and is usually closely linked in partnership, group activities. Friend are very numerous, but friendships are not very enduring. The associates of Libra soon become uncomfortably aware of the fact that they are being adroitly used, that they may not be able to rely too implicitly on the loyalty of the Libran. For, alas, this is the sign of the opportunist. If friends are in trouble, Libra is apt to keep well out of the picture. But nobody can be a more charming, accommodating companion than the Libran when things are going well.

Affinities:

The other two Air signs, Gemini and Aquarius.

French film actress Brigitte Bardot:
Sun in Libra *Black Star*

Antipathies:
Sensitive, intuitive and suspicious Cancer (Water);
Earthy, unimpressionable Capricorn; and, if of the
same sex, Fiery Aries. But Aries and Libra can be
successfully combined in a marriage-link.

Romance and marriage are very important features of the life-history of Libra. Libra is an artiste
in handling love; this type delights in romantic flir-
tation, and usually has a choice of eligible partners.
Marriage most frequently occurs in the middle
twenties; and it may recur later, for if the first
partnership proves unsatisfactory the Libran will
manoeuvre themselves gently out of it into another,

69

more desirable union. But they will also remain on good terms with the ex-partner. Most Librans spend more time out of, than in their homes, being extremely sociable, pleasure-loving. Household arrangements will be rather haphazard, but the home will certainly have a very attractive appearance.

As parents, Librans are easy-going but neglectful, too, of their full responsibilities. They are very apt to lean too much on their children when the latter become adults.

Best Occupations:
This type is well suited for the more elegant, intellectual, artistic and lighter types of profession and occupation. They avoid any kind of work which has physically unpleasant details. Any kind of work which involves acting as go-between, whether it be law, public, relations, salesmanship will appeal. And any occupation which provides plenty of social activity delights the Libran.

There is no strongly ambitious urge for personal distinction; the Libran is always happy to share the limelight, even quite content to remain in the background, so long as he or she benefits from the success of associates.

Handling of money:
No other type can bargain quite as patiently, as shrewdly, as Libra; there is a compulsive urge for gambling due to the instinct for "easy money" (this is not a type which wants to exert itself for anything). Librans are too ready to borrow, and rather too reluctant to discharge their debts.

Physical Constitution and Health:
The constitution is sound, but the nervous system is sensitive, and the general condition of most Librans

is much affected by environment. However, as there is a natural inclination to moderation in all things, little serious health trouble is experienced. This sign rules the kidneys, lumbar region, bloodstream and endocrine glands.

The Life-Pattern of Libra:
Though seldom stable, this is usually fortunate on the whole; for the Libran can turn any circumstances to personal advantage. 24th, 36th and 48th years tend to be especially important ones.

The following are traditionally linked with Libra: the No. 6., all shades of blue, and lighter greens; Friday; Copper; Sapphire and Turquoise.

Cuspal Types: these are the people born in the first five and last five days of the Libra period; they will be less typical because they have something of Virgo or Scorpio in their make-up.

ALL ABOUT SCORPIO— "THE SCORPION"

Classification: 8th sign of the Zodiac, through which the Sun appears to move between, approximately, October 23rd and November 21st of any year.
People born then are Sun-in-Scorpio individuals.
Symbol: ♏
Element: Water.
Quality: Fixed.
Nature: Passive, cold, moist.
Planetary ruler and its Symbol: Mars. (♂)

Appearance:

Height: variable; but in most cases medium, to below average.

Type of body: the trunk is longer than the limbs. Scorpio is a muscular type, with very well shaped joints, well developed calves; the body gives the impression of strength. Head: this is often flat at the top, of average length.

Hair: abundant; usually strong in texture, can be very crisp, wavy; but in those people born in early to mid-November it becomes much finer, straighter. Bodily hair tends to be profuse.

Forehead: strong, broad, of medium height, with very pronounced bone-ridge above eyes; centre of forehead becomes wrinkled. Strong eyebrows, which are straight.

Face: broad, often rather square; strong chin, well-shaped. The cheek-bones are emphasised, so is the jawline. Nose may be either aquiline or concave, and thick at the tip (many Scorpios are discontented with the shape of their noses, and go in for cosmetic surgery.)

The mouth is usually rather thin, very firmly set, serpentine in shape; but here again there is a variation, as one often finds Scorpios with strongly sensual, full-lipped mouths (especially so if born in early November (first week). As with Aries, Scorpio has strong facial lines. The ears are small, the lobes especially so.

The Scorpio neck is very strong, rather short.

Shoulders: broad.

Skin: usually olive, but can be very pale; very opaque.

Teeth not specially distinctive.

Hands: very powerful, with square finger-tips; fingers and palm are evenly proportioned.

Facial expression: serious, very attentive. This is because of the Scorpio eye, which is the most commanding feature. The eyes shine brilliantly, are magnetic, deepset, dark as a rule, but sometimes hazel; they blink far less rapidly than those of other types. Scorpio has the hypnotist's eye.

Voice and manner of speaking: strong tone, compelling note to speech; sometimes a very husky, "sexy" voice.

Movements: deliberate, but never heavy. They give the impression of strong controlled vitality.

Comments on Appearance: There is a special peculiarity about the way in which Scorpio walks; there is a slight swing to this, as though an invisible tail was in motion. The walk can also be sinuous.. The general appearance of Scorpio will always attract attention, though this type make no effort to achieve this.

Scorpios like good clothes and are careful about their appearance. But they dislike ostentation, though they will introduce something exotic into their mode of dress. They select sophisticated styles, but of the best, and sparingly. The women need to be extra careful in choosing the right perfume, as both sexes have a tendency to acid perspiration.

Mannerisms:
Apart from their distinctive way of walking, Scorpios betray no exaggerated mannerisms.

Character:
This is very complex indeed. In Scorpio, intellect and emotion, will and desire fight a perpetual battle. There is something especially indomitable as

well as combative about Scorpio; its stamina being prodigous. Single-mindedness, thoroughness, self-discipline and courage are all emphasised. There is a very self-contained, independent attitude. Organising ability is shown.

Mentality:

Scorpios have extremely introspective, analytical and highly intuitive minds; the urge is to get to the root of everything, and anything which is a mystery intrigues the Scorpio. There is a very marked, but sardonic sense of humour; often there is a very great

French actress Edwige Feuillère:
Sun in Scorpio *David Sim*

love of and talent for Music. Memory is especially keen.

Emotions:
Very intense, and, in the final analysis, the most powerful force in the make-up. But they are kept bottled up, as the Scorpio dislikes showing emotion; though seemingly detached, this type is in fact ultra-sensitive. The fixity of the emotions can be the greatest strength, but also the most dangerous force within Scorpio.

Failings:
Lack of any capacity for compromise. Inordinate, even maniacal jealousy; innate suspicion; a tendency to harbour grievances, to be bitter, vindictive. This type can literally poison itself with its own emotional characteristics. Biting sarcasm, rather than physical retaliation, will be used to defend itself. But Scorpio has a deep conscience, and strives hard to overcome its own failings. Hypercritical of others, it never spares itself.

Relationships:
These are very potent force, but the source of much trouble. First of all, Scorpios seem specially fated to have an unhappy or unfortunate family background, but a sense of duty will keep them tied to the family.

They are highly discriminative in choosing their friends, and very loyal to them. But they also enjoy being alone, as they have plenty of inner resources. They can be much too overbearing, temperamental, possessive in all relationships; but confidences may always be safely entrusted to them (though they seldom reciprocate) as they never betray a secret. The saddest thing about their personal life is their inability to overlook being betrayed by others; even at the cost of intense unhappiness, they will then completely break all association with the betrayer. It is their pride which is their downfall in this respect; for this makes those who would not otherwise be inclined to turn upon them seek to bring them down.

As might be expected, such intimate links as love-affairs, partnerships will always be vivid, but potentially turbulent relationships. However, once the Scorpio regenerates itself, and this is the sign of spiritual regeneration, they make devoted and self-less companions.

The sex-urge is very strong, but kept under control; it can only function happily when there exists a spiritual and mental as well as a purely physical attraction. Scorpio is not promiscuous, but if linked with an unfaithful partner will be driven to frenzy. As parents, Scorpios are strict, but devoted.

Affinities:
The other two Water signs, Cancer and Pisces; also Virgo and in many cases, Capricorn.

Antipathies:
Bombastic Leo, stubborn Taurus (if of the same sex; as marriage-partners, they make a happy, mutually fulfilling couple); erratic Aquarius.

Best Occupations:
Those which demand both intellectual skill and manual strength or stamina. Professions of a humane, and analytical kind; surgery, psychiatry. The Defence Services; anything connected with engineering, physics, genetics or biology. But there is often great dramatic ability.

In commerce, anything to do with handling of

other people's financial interests; banking; insurance; stockbroking; accountancy.

As this is the 8th house sign, morticians are to be found in this group.

Lastly, the Church or law; both professions have a special attraction for Scorpio.

Handling of money:
Scorpio is prudent, but not mean, about money. Money for its own sake makes no appeal to Scorpio, who will work tirelessly at very unremunerative jobs which absorb his interest. This sign does, however, tend to inherit money or possessions—or else the debts of relatives!

As regards the preferable status, independence is the thing for which Scorpios crave; they are also very capable in responsible positions. Partnerships of a working nature will probably be fortunate, materially, but test Scorpio greatly. One specially notable characteristic is that, being single minded, the Scorpio always knows what career it wishes to follow, and will do so even if it has to achieve it only after delays, or by devious means.

Physical Constitution and Health:
This is a very wiry sign, and it also has a strong constitution. But Scorpio will drive itself to the limits of endurance, and can collapse under acute emotional strain. But recuperative powers are very good, and very rapid. This type struggles hardest to combat the final defeat—death. The parts of the body ruled by Scorpio are the sex-organs; but the throat, tonsils and thyroid gland are also very vulnerable. Most Scorpios acquire scars on their hands.

The Life-Pattern of Scorpio:
Very active, very combative, and usually very suc-

cessful in the latter part of life. 27th, 36th and 63rd years are important milestones.

The following are traditionally linked with Scorpio: the No. 9; deeper shades of red; Tuesday; Iron; the Ruby; Bloodstone.

Cuspal types: these are the people born in the first five and last five days of the Scorpio period, who are less typical because they have something of Libra or Sagittarius in their make-up.

ALL ABOUT SAGITTARIUS— "THE ARCHER"

Classification: 9th sign of the Zodiac, through which the Sun appears to move between, approximately, November 22nd and December 20th of any year. People born then are Sun-in-Sagittarius individuals.

Symbol: ♐

Element: Fire.

Quality: Cardinal.

Nature: Positive, hot and dry.

Planetary ruler and its Symbol: Jupiter (♃)

Appearance:

Height: average to tall.

Type of Body: long limbs in proportion to the trunk; very loose-limbed type. Everything about the Sagittarian tends to be a little on the large side, including the general build. In youth, very slim in figure; but a bit portly from the early forties onwards. The body is muscular.

Head: long in shape (horsey); the crown is very high, and arched. Hair: fine in texture, plentiful.

Forehead: very high and with an arch to it. Wider at upper corners and also at base; gives the Sagittarian a brainy look. The brows are fine and curved.

Face: full, and long. Large, prominent nose, with flaring nostrils, and thick at the tip. The mouth is wide, but with well-shaped lips. The eyes are large, almond-shaped, and tilt at the corners. The irises are usually very light in colour. Laughter-lines appear early at the corners of the eyes. Strong jaw and chin. The neck is quite slender, but strong; shoulders are surprisingly narrow, and have a slope to them; and many Sagittarians have stooping figures.

Skin: very healthy, but with open pores.

Teeth: very large, especially the two middle ones in top row.

Hands: large, well-made, with long, tapering fingers. Feet also very long, very slim.

Facial expression: very frank, good-humoured.

Voice and manner of speaking: the voice of the Sagittarian has an equine element, for when they laugh it can sound like a whinny. The timbre of the voice is full-toned, and the manner of speech a little slow, thoughtful.

Movements: very free, energetic; there is a swing to the walk.

Comments on Appearance: the appearance changes very much as time goes by. In youth, the Sagittarian has a "rangy" look; in middle age the deportment becomes much more dignified, the figure be-

British television personality Cliff Michelmore:
Sun in Sagittarius

comes much fuller; the look of quizzical good humour becomes a benevolent gaze.

Sagittarians are a sporty type, and look their best in country clothes or sports-wear; they love tweeds, hate constricting clothing. Even the women seem to prefer jewellery which is slightly "sporty" and the type which is the insignia of clubs, societies. Being conventional, the Sagittarian will always appear correctly dressed for any formal occasion.

Mannerisms:

Are all equine. Head-tossing when surprised or annoyed; restless movements of the feet when bored.

Character:

The Sagittarian character is a very pleasant one; idealistic, honest, philosophical. There is a tremendous desire for freedom and progress, and a very highly developed sense of justice. An adventurous as well as an ambitious streak, impulsivenes, versatility, organising flair—are all characteristics.

Mentality:

Inspirational, intuitive to some extent, too: for this type has keen foresight. Optimism, the instinct to think and act big are truly Sagittarian traits. As a rule there is a natural inclination towards academic, religious and philosophical subjects. Sagittarians have a very jovial sense of humour.

Emotions:

Very much on the surface, but very exuberant. Emotionally, however, Sagittarians "blow hot and cold" by turns; even in romantic attachments, passion is not sustained for long.

Failings:

Impatience; extravagance; ambivalence; lack of concentration and continuity; tendency towards exaggeration, not only mentally but in tastes, habits, behaviour generally. There is something of the gambler in Sagittarius; and too often the Archer will shoot his bow far wide of the mark. Because in the temperament there is a conflict (usual in dual signs) between respect for convention and freedom-loving inclinations, Sagittarians can be rather illogical, hypocritical. And there is a snobbish streak which makes them too condescending.

Relationships:

Sagittarius likes to trace back its family tree to find out whether there have been any distinguished branches thereon. Relationships with relatives—and inlaws—are usually very cordial.

Extremely friendly, Sagittarius makes many links, socially; loves joining clubs, societies, and loves to be connected with influential or affluent people; but is very kind to his poorer, obscure cronies. They are wonderful dispensers of hospitality, born raconteurs. The attitude towards friends is sincere, helpful.

In romantic and marital attachments the Sagittarian is less reliable. They are all flirts by instinct, usually have two romances on hand simultaneously; marry early but often marry twice; or, if not, discreetly form an attachment elsewhere which is long-lasting.

Domesticity is seldom a virtue; the Sagittarian likes to have two homes, and to travel a great deal. Even when tethered in one place, will spend more time with friends, in clubs, than in the house. Children are given much freedom, but also a very good education.

Affinities:
The other two Fire signs, Aries and Leo.

Antipathies:
Airy Gemini, Mutable Virgo and Watery Pisces. However, Sagittarius often marries Gemini; but as both are inclined to second unions, the link-up is likely to be short-lived.

Best Occupations:
The academic, scientific and spiritual professions; but in particular the Law, or the political world. The Defence Services also attract Sagittarius, and so does any occupation which involves extensive travel, has to do with Sport and the open-air life, animals. Sagittarians have a specially close connec-

tion with all activities to do with Racing—including bookmaking.

This type is prone to change careers around the age of thirty, or else to follow two different ones simultaneously. A great many live and work abroad.

Partnerships are successful, and so are any large-scale undertakings carried on by Sagittarius; it is when their circumstances are cramped, their interests and activities on a small scale, that failure is likeliest. They revel in totally independent action.

Handling of money:
Money will be spent prodigally; but Sagittarius is lucky in attracting it to himself. This type is also lucky in litigation.

Physical Constitution and Health:
The Sagittarian enjoys good health because this is a very robust type. But the nervous system is very highly charged; and this is an accident-prone type. Sagittarius is the sign connected with the liver, the hepatic system, the hips, thighs; but the respiratory system is often sensitive.

One or two other very interesting things should be mentioned regarding the Sagittarian. This type dreams particularly vividly, and often in colour; the dreams are truly prophetic, too. There is a particular fondness for and skill in mountaineering; and when forced to live or work in close surroundings the Sagittarians develop claustrophia very quickly. And, in the case of Sagittarius, it is certainly true that things "happen in threes".

The Life-Pattern of Sagittarius:
Very adventurous and very colourful for most of the time; the 30th year is probably the most outstanding turning point therein.

The following are traditionally linked with Sagittarius; the Number 3; violet and purple; Thursday; the Amethyst; Tin.

Cuspal Types: these are the people born in the first five and last five days of the Sagittarius period; they are more sober in outlook, more moderate in behaviour, because they have something of Scorpio or Capricorn in their make-up.

ALL ABOUT CAPRICORN— "THE GOAT"

Classification: 10th sign of the Zodiac, through which the Sun appears to move between, approximately, December 21st and January 19th of any year. People born then are Sun-in-Capricorn individuals.
Symbol: V^3
Element: Earth.
Quality: Cardinal.
Nature: Passive, dry, cold.
Planetary ruler and its Symbol: Saturn (♄)

Appearance:

Height: usually above average; but a short variety is born around the first week of January.

Type of Body: angular as a rule, very sinewy; bones and joints large and prominent; bones may be brittle, as the calcium-content can be below average. But the bone-structure of this type can be its best feature; this is why many Capricornians are beautiful, or handsome, in an austere way in later life. This type, incidentally, looks older than its years.

Head: upper part well developed. Head is long.

Hair: strong in growth, coarse to the touch; straight; usually very dark, sometimes black. Body has a lot of hair.

Forehead: that of a thinker; deep-lined, protruding, full just above the nose. Eyebrows are plentiful, but not well shaped. Face: deeply indented with lines, giving furrowed cheeks in quite early life, ageing. Eyes are deepset, dark in colour, sometimes small and dull. Nose is long, sometimes hooked, and the mouth small, thin, severe in expression; in some individuals, there is a slightly protruding underlip. The jawline is long, the chin firm, protruding. Ears are large, very gristly, angular, but flat rather than curved. The neck is long and corded.

Shoulders: rather broad, square.

Skin: somewhat taut; sallow, thick in texture; but skin-ailments are very common to this type, due to excessive acid or dryness.

Feet: large, but poor in quality.

Hands: large, hard to the touch; very pronounced knuckles; a worker's and also a thinker's hand.

Facial expression: very serious, often stern or sad-looking. The shape of face, the lines on it all contribute to this impression. So does the downward gaze.

Voice and way of speaking: varies; can be loud, harsh; or else very thin in tone. This is anything but a locquacious type as a rule; speech tends to be slow, very matter-of-fact.

Movements: slow; a heavy-footed type; slightly clumsy in motion.

Comments on Appearance: something of the goat can be traced in the appearance of the Capricorn, especially in the older men, who may sport the true goatee beard.

As a rule, Capricorn is not fashion conscious and is indifferent to what it is wearing. When any interest in clothes is exhibited, the taste will be traditional. There is a preference for darker colours, sensible garments, and, in the women, antique jewellery. Clothes are fully worn out before being discarded.

Former Chancellor of Federal German Republic Conrad Adenauer: Sun in Capricorn *Horst Tappe*

Mannerisms:

Nothing very conspicious about these; this is not a restless type the lack of mobility strikes one most.

Character:

Very consistent in its strength, single-mindedness, realistic approach to life. Capricornians are tenacious, orthodox, logical, conservative, conventional. But also ambitious. The urge for security is very emphasised and influences all they do. Very industrious by nature, and very good at organising, also extremely conscientious.

Mentality:

Studious, serious, reflective, introspective. Imagination is almost always completely lacking; sense of humour may also be absent but, if not, it is dry wit. The one artistic attribute of this sign is its love of music. Mental reflexes are slow, but the memory is very retentive. Interests are very limited; the Capricornian becomes a specialist in one field.

Emotions:

Though this seems a very phlegmatic type, Capricorn is in reality capable of deep fidelity to those it respects or loves. The sex-urge is quite strong, too, but functions spasmodically; mainly because the energy of this type is forced into other directions. But Capricornians are not sentimental or romantic in their emotional approach. On the other hand, they have a strong attachment to their family; and the family may demand far too much of Capricorn.

Failings:

These are summed up by the limitations of the type. Inflexibility; obstinacy; intolerance; bigotry; pessimism; acquisitiveness; a lack of sensibility; lack of diplomacy.

Relationships:

The true Capricornian is rather anti-social; loves solitude; confines its attention to other members of the family and a few family friends. Even when sociably inclined, Capricorn is shy and gauche in company, slow to form attachments. But once friendships are formed, they last. Capricornians are more attracted to older people than those of their own age, or younger.

Capricorn loves with the head as much as the heart; and takes time to make up its mind about marriage. But this may be because of material considerations; usually Capricorn can't afford to marry early. The sad thing about Capricorn is that it is willing to sacrifice true love for the sake of a good marriage. Marriage may be with an older partner, or a childhood sweetheart. In middle age something odd happens to the Capricornian — of both sexes; they begin to act like the giddy goat; but they don't extend these capers over a very long period.

A domesticated type which clings to its home-life and resents any intrusion on the privacy of this. Much sacrifice is willingly made on behalf of children, but the inability to be emotionally demonstrative, the instinct to be too strict, impairs relationships between children and parents.

Affinities:

The two other Earth types, Taurus and Virgo; also Scorpio.

Antipathies:

Fiery Aries, Airy Libra. And, contrary to the usual rule, marriage between Capricorn and Cancer seldom works out too well. When of the same sex, there is a very strong antipathy between these two.

Best Occupations:

Those which are very solid, very safe; and those which demand long, labourious routine work of an unexciting kind. Capricorn is not seeking glamour, adventure or a challenge from its working activities. It is just working steadily, patiently towards security and freedom. For this reason, it will gravitate into Commerce because Commerce offers best rewards financially. If opportunity allows the Capricorn to work alone there will be much greater satisfaction.

Governement Service; education; anything related to building, architecture, mining, farming and engineering are specially suitable activities.

Success will be achieved, no matter what the odds; but it is almost always attained the hard way. If it comes early, there is danger of downfall in middle life; and recovery will be very slow.

Attitude to money:

Frugal. Capricornians can exist on the minimum; always save as soon as possible, and then invest very shrewdly. Not prone to gambling; not at all generous, except to relatives, to whom they will, if necessary, yield up every penny they possess.

Physical Constitution and Health:

This type may be rather sickly in early years; but gets tougher as it grows older; and lives to be an octogenerian, sometimes a centagenerian. The digestive system is poor; and this type often has difficulty in putting on any weight. Eliminatve functions are also sluggish. There is too much acidity in the system. Blood-pressure is low, but the arteries harden in later life; the pulse is very slow.

Capricorn is connected with the knees, the bone-framework of the body, and the skin.

The Life-Pattern of Capricorn:
A history of struggle against adversity of one kind or another; but a history with a very successful climax. It is the Capricornian who comes to the fore when others are preparing to retire. The elder statesman type, in fact. 60 is almost always a fortunate turning point in the life.

The following are traditionally linked with Capricorn; the number 8; deep browns, black; Saturday; Lead; Black Pearl and Dark Sapphire.

Cuspal Types: these are the people born in the first five and last five days of the Capricorn period; they will be less typical because of their having something of Sagittarius or Aquarius in their make-up.

ALL ABOUT AQUARIUS— "THE WATER-BEARER"

Classification: 11th sign of the Zodiac, through which the Sun appears to move between, approximately, January 20th and February 18th of any year. People born then are Sun-in-Aquarius individuals.

Symbol: ≈

Element: Air.

Quality: Fixed.

Nature: Positive, moist, sanguine.

Planetary ruler and its Symbol: Uranus (♅)

Saturn is also traditionally linked with this sign. (♄)

Appearance:
Height: there are two very different types; one is very tall, slim; the other shorter, thickset; one is blonde, the other dark in colouring.

Type of body: in both types, the trunk is long, flexible and the bone-structure on the large side.

Head: short and of an odd shape, rather like a round tower; the lower part of the back of the head is strongly emphasised.

Hair: very good in texture, wavy, shining; full of electricity.

Forehead: full in the upper part but concave in the middle. Brows are well shaped, slightly curved.

Face: the features are finely etched, giving refinement to a face which is broad, with angular cheekbones, and triangular towards the chin. The mouth is firmly shut, but seems to be half-smiling even in repose. When the smile breaks loose, it is a particularly radiant one. In fact, radiance comes out very strongly from the Aquarian. The eyes, in particular, which are wide-open in gaze, are lighted up from within; and they seem to be laughing. There are slight pouches under the eyes. The distinctive thing about the nose, apart from its clearcut lines, is that it has no indentation between it and the forehead; it is the true Greek nose. There is a strong jawline; and the chin is firm, pointed, slightly protruding. The neck is short and thick.

Shoulders: square, broad.

Skin: very good; delicate in appearance, rather pale, slightly shiny—and porous.

Teeth: well shaped, but not too strong.

Hands: very refined hand; long, strong fingers; tapering at the tips.

Feet are also long and slim.

Facial expression: very benign, but rather detached.

Voice and way of speaking: the voice is very clear, and the speech rapid, disjointed, staccato.

Movements: disjointed; rather galvanic; reminiscent of a clockwork figure brought to life.

Comments on Appearance: there is something arresting about the Aquarian appearance, because one is alerted by it. The spontaneity with which the Aquarian does, or says things, the unexpectedness of their conversation, movements, and something distinctive about what they wear arrests attention.

With regard to clothes the Aquarian approach is a bit peculiar. No fashion is followed slavishly; the Aquarian adds his or her own distinctive additons to this, or else flouts it completely. The oddest assortment of garments, the most unsuitable form of dress, may be selected; yet there is something especially fascinating about the result. Sheer perversity will make the Aquarian appear in shabby or otherwise unsuitable clothes at a formal function.

Mannerisms:
Deliberate eccentricity. A dislike of being touched other than by the people to whom they are closely attached.

Character:
Very distinctive. The Aquarian is the individualist of the zodiac; the one who not only thinks, acts differently, but who has a flair for turning what is dull, or familiar, into something new and exciting. Very good organising ability, tremendous enthusiasm, tenacity, strength of will and of completely detached and objective attitude to life are Aquarian characteristics. This is the type that outgrows everything and everyone in time, the type which must ever go forward, carrying others along with it. This is not an egocentric type, either; for there is a very strong humanitarian urge in all Aquarians.

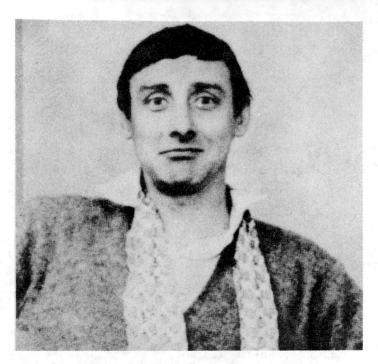

Irish comedian and writer Spike Milligan:
Sun in Aquarius

Another characteristic is the spasmodic way in which
the Aquarian functions, mentally, emotionally and
physically.

Mentality:
Very creative and inspirational; also deeply reflective and introspective. The Aquarian has a wonderful sense of humour.

Emotions:
There is a sensuous rather than sensual emotional
attitude. Emotions in this type are refined by intelligence, discrimination. Aquarians are capable of
very deep attachments; but are always objective
about the people they love or admire.

The family life and the romantic life alike are
odd; Aquarians often break away from the family

altogether, if only temporarily; they are usually the "odd man out" in the family circle, anyhow.

Where romance is concerned, Aquarius gives not a fig for the conventions; but this does not mean promiscuity. It is merely a question of following the dictates of its own heart. A union is likely to be more successful and lasting if it is irregular rather than legalised. If a partnership is broken, the Aquarian becomes completely oblivious of the other person concerned.

The home-life of Aquarius is conducted on erratic lines; children are brought up on ultra-modern methods, but adore their unpossessive parents.

Friendships are those which allow the Aquarian not to become too intimately involved with the people concerned; they prefer groups of friends rather than close individual tie-ups.

Affinities:
The two other Air types, Gemini and Libra.

Antipathies:
Earthy Taurus, Watery Scorpio. The traditional attraction of opposites will bring Leos and Aquarians of opposite sex together, but unions are not likely to be permanent. Those Leos who are of the same sex as Aquarius are completely rebuffed.

Failings:
Contrariness; the instinct to go off abruptly at a complete tangent when conditions become a strain; unpredictability — the Aquarian never even knows himself how he will act in any emergency. Sudden changes of outlook which are made over-rapidly.

Best Occupations:
Anything that is wildly out-of-the-ordinary, for one thing. And the professions for preference, too,

because Aquarius prefers a vocation to money-making. All types of intellectual or humane activity; anything to do with electricity, science politics.

The preference is for a lone-wolf career; but if this is impossible Aquarius excels in organising others, and cannot tolerate a humdrum job.

Handling of Money:
Paradoxical. The Aquarian is generous over big things, niggardly over small ones. Will dispense its generosity to those who have least call upon it, and be inconsiderate to those who should be helped. Money is freely given to any kind of charity.

Physical Constitution and Health:
Aquarius has a strong constitution and long life-expectation; suffers little illness. The nervous system is well controlled; but under great duress can break down. This sign of the zodiac has to do with the circulatory system, arteries, veins, ankles.

The Life-Pattern of Aquarius:
Reads much more fascinatingly than any work of fiction, it is so episodic, spectacular. Opportunities and setbacks occur when and whence least expected. When at the peak of success, Aquarius will relinquish everything to go in search of new stimulus; and when everything seems to be at its worst there will be a meteoric change for good. Alternate 4 and 10 year cycles seem to be the general rule of experience.

The following are traditionally linked with Aquarius; the Number 4, blue-greens; Friday; the Opal and Aquamarine; Uranium.

Cuspal Types: these are the people born in the first five and last five days of the Aquarius period; they will be less typical because they have something of Capricorn or Pisces in their make-up.

ALL ABOUT PISCES—"THE FISHES"

Classification: 12th sign of the Zodiac, through which the Sun appears to move between, approximately, February 19th and March 20th of any year. People born then are Sun-in-Pisces individuals.

Symbol: ♓

Element: Water.

Quality: Mutable (Common).

Nature: Passive, cold, moist.

Planetary ruler and its Symbol: Neptune ♆

Personally, I am positive that Neptune is the predominant ruler of Pisces, although Jupiter (♃) is linked with this sign.

Appearance:

Height: more often than not, below average; but there is a minority which is tall.

Type of Body: fleshy, with a pear-like shape to the trunk. Limbs are disproportionately short and not too well formed; feet are splayed, and there is usually some irregularity, or deformity, about them.

Head: large and high in shape.

Hair: fine to the touch, grows downward rather than upward; profuse, but apt to thin out early in life. Of a darker rather than lighter colour. Many born under this sign have a double crown of hair.

Forehead: full and wide, especially in lower half. High crown to forehead. Eyebrows are arched. The eyes are usually large, often very beautiful, soulful, or dreamy; and there is a high proportion of green-eyed people in this type. But there is also a type of

Piscean with beautiful, large but very sly-looking, secretive eyes. Cheeks are exceptionally full, bulbous. The Pisces nose is soft, fleshy, sometimes concave. The mouth can be very loose-lipped, fishlike, or else extremely sensitive, with a protruding upper lip. Features seem to be small because the face is rather large, and either heart-shaped or flat and platelike. Ears are round, a little flabby. The neck is short, full.

Shoulders: tend to be round, and sloping; they appear to be narrow because of the trunk's pear-like shape.

Skin: pale, flaccid.

Teeth: not too strong.

Hands: very soft to the touch, cone-shaped and with thick, short fingers; the inner part of the hand is cushiony.

American film actress Elizabeth Taylor: Sun in Pisces

Facial Expression: usually rather abstracted.

Voice and manner of speaking: deep and soft voice, speech tending to tail off, leaving sentences unfinished. Many Pisceans have speech impediments.

Movements: Pisceans do not have a good carriage; they either shuffle along, or edge their way along sideways. But occasionally one finds the type which is particularly fluid, and rhythmic in motion; they are the people born in the latter part of the period.

Comments on Appearance: in silhouette, there is a very definite fishlike outline.

Pisceans like clothes, especially loosely fitting ones; and they can look very attractive; but they seldom achieve real chic. However carefully groomed, tailored, the Piscean seems to be slightly shabby; clothes quickly go limp on them. This type suffer agonies with their feet, and so cling to shoes which are disreputuable, down-at-heel. At the first opportunity, they will change from walking shoes into slippers, or go barefoot. A sure sign that the Piscean is deeply disturbed emotionally is when they let their appearance go to pieces.

Mannerisms:

These change rapidly because the Piscean is so impressionable that he or she instinctively imitates the people they are in contact with. Similarly, note how the facial expression will change when in varied company. The Piscean is something of a chameleon.

Character:

Very introvert; very malleable, and completely dominated by the emotional attitude. Basically, Pisceans are idealistic, altruistic, the most well-meaning people in the world. But this is the sign of self-destruction as well as self-salvation; and it is true that Pisces is his own worst enemy. These people are so many sided, so versatile, so "fluid" as it were — all because of a compulsive urge to be a part of everything around them — that they defy complete classification.

Mentality:

Highly intuitive and very imaginative. Many very clever mathematicians are born under this sign, and also people who have tremendous capacity for highly abstract, involved thinking; yet it seems to be instinct rather than logic that guides them to their conclusions. The aesthetic sense is well developed, giving a keen reaction to the Arts, especially to music, poetry and painting. Memory is poor.

Emotions:

These are all-embracing, with one exception; the Piscean does not experience sheer rage. Emotionally, Pisces is sentimental, very affectionate, very romantic, and very sensation-seeking. Moods alternate from one extreme to the other. No two people who are in contact with Pisces will ever get the same impression about this type.

Failings:

Escapism is the chief of these; for basically Pisces is very timid the other great handicap is self-indulgence. Weakness of character is usual in a very large proportion of people born under this sign; and this leads to vacillation, procrastination, prevarication. Yet poor Pisces is always willing to try to mend his ways; it is a case of the spirit being eager, but the flesh too frail.

Relationships:

Always highly involved, both in and outside the family circle. Much attached to relatives, Pisces is a continual worry to them. Friends and relatives alike are always rescuing the Piscean from various foolish predicaments of their own engineering.

Pisces is so easily influenced—and too often by the wrong type of companions, who will batten on this type. Everyone is fond of Pisces, but everyone is driven to distraction at some time or other by "The Fish".

Romance and marriage are of course prominent features of the life-history. Love affairs are numerous but a lot of them are kept under cover — both before and after marriage. This is one of the signs which is apt to make the wrong marriage, marry more than once, or seek consolation outside marriage.

As a parent, nobody could be more kind, more well-intentioned; but it is the children who have to take their Piscean parents in hand from time to time.

The Piscean home is delightful to be in; warm, friendly, very untidy as a rule, but essentially "lived in".

Affinities:

The other two Water signs, Cancer and Scorpio. And also Libra; for Venus, the planetary ruler of that sign, is "Exalted" in Pisces; and in this one instance the significance of "Exaltation" is clearly shown. But alas, when brought into close relationship these two, though on the best of terms, do little to help each other, but rather encourage each other's weaknesses.

Antipathies:

Airy Gemini, Fiery Sagittarius, and Virgo; for though in most cases opposites are well matched in marriage, in that of Virgo and Pisces no relationship can ever lead to success or satisfaction.

Best Occupations:

The Piscean can fit into almost any occupation; but is temperamentally more suited for the professions, especially the humane or spiritual professions. These encourage the Piscean to develop all that is highest in their natures, to combat the weaknesses. They will exert themselves in order to be of help to others, whereas on their own account they will make no great efforts. Other occupations which especially attract the Piscean are the glamorous ones connected with the Arts, entertainment and they also naturally gravitate into anything to do with fluids, marine life. Academic occupations of the more abstruse kind also attract them; for though impractical in the daily affairs of life, they are wonderful theorists.

This is not a type adapted to, or inclined to work alone, though they may work in secluded surroundings and behind the scenes, for there is no great desire to be a public figure.

Handling of Money:

As an economist, Pisces has wonderful theories about the management of money. In handling his own finances, the Piscean invariably gets everything into a mess. Most Pisceans are extremely careless and generous with money; but there is one type which goes to the other extreme and brings thrift to the point of miserliness. An element of luck always gets Pisces out of its difficulties in the nick of time.

Physical Constitution and Health:

The Pisces type have an absorbent constitution, and they are rather susceptible to ailments if in the company of ailing people. This is the one handicap which baulks them when they associate themselves with medical work. But it is self-indulgence which plays most havoc with Piscean health; they should try to be abstemious as regards liquor, smoking, eating — and as regards their sex-habits, too. All react acutely on the generally standard of health.

This sign of the zodiac is connected with the glandular system as a whole, but in particular the pituitary; the appendix; bowels; feet. Pisceans are very responsive to drugs, and should be cautious about taking even the very mild type of drug-pills; they are the anaesthetist's best patients. And they are very susceptible to food, and especially shellfish, poisoning.

The life-pattern of Pisces:
Chaotic, and rather pathetic. So many golden opportunities are lost. Yet the wonderful, the most endearing thing about the Piscean is their willingness to try, try again; no-one could be too harsh with them. for all their backsliding, when one remembers that they are their own victims; and one can greatly admire the way in which the Pisces will sacrifice itself wholly for the sake of a true love of its fellow-man.

The following are traditionally linked with Pisces; the number 7; (to some extent also 3); mauve; sea-green; lilac; Thursday and Friday; Neptunium; the Aquamarine, the Emerald.

Cuspal Types; these are the people born in the first five and last five days of the Pisces period; they will be less typical than the rest having something of Aquarius or Aries in their make-up. The most strong-willed, capable, successful Pisceans, who in many ways seem to contradict what has been written of the type in general, tend to be born around the second week of March.

4: THE HOROSCOPE:
HOUSES, SIGNS AND PLANETS

THE horoscope is not only the means by which the astrologer charts the positions of Sun, Moon and planets in the zodiac at any specific moment in time in relation to any particular place of reference, but also the medium by which the potentialities of that moment in time in connection with the character and destiny of an individual, the fate of a country, the result of a war, the kind of harvest which will be forthcoming, or anything else it is expedient to enquire about, can be deduced.

The Horoscope is simply the Greek name, derived from words which mean "Hour" (or time) and "Watcher" for the map made of the heavens at this moment. Its focal point of importance is the degree of the ecliptic (the zodiac) which is on the eastern horizon of the place of observation, the place where the event, such as the birth of a child, occurs, and horoscope came to be interpreted as "the house of the Ascendant."

The horoscope consists of twelve sections, or houses as they are called, which are in accordance with the symbolic meanings of the *constellations* of the zodiac. Nowadays, of course, they correspond to the twelve *signs* of the zodiac.

Next in importance to the Ascendant house (first house) comes the Midheaven of the horoscope-chart— the Upper Meridian section of the heavens. The houses directly opposite these two, which are, respectively the Descendant (the seventh house) and the nadir, the lower Meridian (fourth house) are also important. They are the "angular houses" of the horoscope, its "Cardinal Points".

Those houses which follow them (second, fifth, eighth and eleventh) are called the "Succedent" houses. And the remaining four (third, sixth, ninth and twelfth) are the "Cadent" houses in the horoscope.

In any horoscope, the various signs of the zodiac will be found in different positions on the "Cusps" (the starting-points) of each houses, but, of course, following their natural order; so that if Leo, say, is on the cusp of the 1st house, and does not also extend into the second (which it can do, for reasons which will be explained later) Virgo must be on the cusp of that house.

The particular sign on the horizon, and therefore the sequence of signs through the various houses will, of course, depend on the date, time and place connected the event in question – in this case, the birth of a child; for in this book we shall be concentrating on nativities.

The houses in which Sun, Moon and planets are placed are especially important; but even when a house is unoccupied, it has a meaning in connection with some aspect life; for the sign on its cusp and the planet ruling that sign have to be considered.

Now, one last point about the houses. Each has its "opposite number" (such as 1 and 7, 2 and 8 and so on). You will notice how the meanings of these opposites have something in common, and this is because the first of the two has a limited, subjective interpretation, whereas the other has an expanded, objective interpretation of similar attributes refer to the development of the individual within himself and in his immediate environment and to his connections with the world at large.

THE FIRST HOUSE

This is related to the physical appearance and the personality, as distinct from the character, of the person concerned. Whichever sign is on the cusp of this house will show itself in build, looks; and, if there is also a planet or planets in this house, and particularly if they are close to the degree rising, they also will leave their signature.

Should the person be born at sunrise, the sun-sign will be on this house; in which case, as the sun-sign denotes the inherent character, the real ego of the person, personality and character will be united. The individual will also be more easy to recognise as a specimen of his sun-sign.

Temperament, mannerisms and to some extent the general condition of health will also be revealed by sign and planets in this part of the horoscope.

THE SECOND HOUSE

This represents the materialistic instincts; the financial aspects of the person's affairs. It shows the earning capacity, and the likely way in which money will be earned, and also such assets as have any monetary value, the personal possessions of the individual.

THE THIRD HOUSE

This is connected with the communicative faculties of the person; in other words, it reveals the type of mentality, the kinds of things that will mentally appeal to the person.

But it is also the house connected with those people with whom the person is brought into close communication through circumstances and i.e., relatives (other than the parents) neighbours.

Again, it relates to physical communications as regards travelling, but applies to short journeys, those habitual to daily life, those confined to nearby places.

THE FOURTH HOUSE

This is concerned with the roots of the person; his home, his family in general, but the parents in particular. It gives a clue to any hereditary characteristics; describes the domestic pattern of the subject, the circumstances in which he was reared.

THE FIFTH HOUSE

This has to do with physical creativity in relation to the personal side of the life. Thus, it denotes love-affairs (first step towards marriage and the creation of a home and family); children, entertainment and methods of seeking entertainment (via hobbies, or methods of pleasurable diversion).

THE SIXTH HOUSE

This house deals with the industry of the native (as the old astrologers called the subject of the horoscope), his obligations to others. It is the house of service. The conditions of the working environment, or the people who work for the subject, are indicated.

But it is also the house of health, suggesting the general condition of health, the types of ailments likely, and the causes of illhealth.

THE SEVENTH HOUSE

Whereas the first house dealt with the person himself, the seventh denotes his close relationships with other people outside the family circle. Thus, it is the house of partnerships, but also of adversaries, competitors; it is related to those people to whom the subject must adjust himself outside the limits of his family.

THE EIGHTH HOUSE

Whereas the second house dealt with the person's own financial affairs, this house is concerned with the way in which he is affected by other people's finances, his benefits from, and his obligations to them. So it covers legacies, the finances of partners, financial exchanges such as loans, payments.

But the eighth house is also connected with the chain of experience covered by life-and-death cycles; it is the house of death and regeneration, fundamental reorganisation, either materially, physically or even emotionally.

THE NINTH HOUSE

Whereas the third house dealt with limited communications, the ninth has to do with the extension of these. Mentally, therefore, it is linked up with capacity for and inclination towards, religion, philosophy, what the person can aspire to mentally.

Then again, it is correlated with extended travel; and with relatives gained through marriage.

THE TENTH HOUSE

The fourth house symbolises the person's base; his home, family-unit. Its opposite, the tenth house, is concerned with his major activities outside the home, his career. Whereas the sixth house signifies what he owes, as it were, to others, the tenth will show what he can wrest from the world at large in the way of prestige, material gains. To some extent it also signifies his ideals, but his *practical* ideals.

THE ELEVENTH HOUSE

Whereas the fifth house was concerned with the limited, individual creativity, in a pleasurable sense, of the subject (his children, hobbies, ways of self-entertainment) the eleventh house denotes pleasures gained through wider communication of this kind; the stimulus gained from friendships, group activities. This house also has to do with the realisation of the yearnings of the person, his hopes; but more from the social than the material angle. The pleasures and benefits derived from this house have to be shared on a wider scale, as the give-and-take of friendship implies.

THE TWELFTH HOUSE

This rules everything that is obscure, but links up also with things connected with the sixth house. It indicates charity – given or received; duty – carried to the point of personal sacrifice; health – that of other people whose circumstances affect the subject.

Whereas the sixth house has to do with the people who are the colleagues, or the subordinates (employees) of the subject of the horoscope, the twelfth house has to do with those who work against him secretly – his *hidden* enemies.

But it also has to do with the enemy within the subject himself, the weaknesses, not of body but of character which can bring him to destruction; and it is concerned also with his unconscious, over which he has no control because he is not aware of it.

Signs and Houses

Harking back to the division of the zodiac into Elements and Qualities, note carefully the link-up between these and the houses of the horoscope; thus:

ELEMENTS

Fire signs; (Aries, Leo, Sagittarius) natural rulers of the first, fifth and ninth houses of the Horoscope, which rule the creative forces, the vitality of the individual, and through which the vitality is directed, expansively, positively, into physical action (Self 1st) reproduction (creation of children 5th) extension of mental and spiritual faculties and physical extension, through uprooting from familiar surroundings (travel 9th).

Earth signs: (Taurus, Virgo, Capricorn) natural rulers of second, sixth and tenth houses, those parts of the horoscope concerned with activity related to the material needs of the subject: money, work, status in life.

Air signs: (Gemini, Libra, Aquarius) natural rulers of the "lines of communication" between the subject and the people around him, and ruling relatives, partners and friends.

Water signs: (Cancer, Scorpio, Pisces) natural rulers of the life-death cycle of experience and the secrets concerned with this, the forces through which the survival of the individual is ensured or imperilled; his home (fourth) his physical degeneration (death) his physical and psychological perils (actions of hidden enemies, dangers of the unconscious).

QUALITIES

Cardinal: connected with the signs which are the natural rulers of the first, fourth, seventh and tenth houses, mediums which provide the means as well as the stimulus for the projection of the person's vital energies; the home, relationships with the world at large and with partners in particular, and the career. They also define the boundaries of this possible scope of physical control over circumstance.

Fixed: connected with the signs which are natural rulers of the second, fifth, eighth and eleventh houses, areas of activity which will determine the extent of the person's security, and the after-effects of his existence; thus, they are concerned with acquisition of material resources (money, possessions) acquistion of children, degeneration and regeneration of material and physical resources (the eighth house has to do with legacies, monetary support as it were, and also with the regeneration of flagging physical resources); friendships (through which the person will be remembered outside the family circle, through which his actions will be perpetuated beyond the sphere of purely personal effects).

Cardinal: connected with the third, sixth, ninth and twelfth houses and their natural sign-rulers. The state of flux that is inevitable in all life-conditions, and the factors in life-experience which most exercise the adaptive capacity of the person, first mentally (third house) then physically (effects of health-conditions of a personal nature); then the impersonal, or extended conditions of flux, demanding adaptation to factors beyond the control of the person, such as totally unfamiliar surroundings, exploration mentally into the no-man's land of spiritual and philosophical speculation, effects produced by the health conditions – or machinations – of other people over whom the person has neither control or knowledge. They are as it were the areas of the horoscope, the factors of life which most endanger the potential security of the person because they are unrelated to his own control over life-forces, or to his limited control thereof.

The combination of signs and houses

The particular sign which extends over the boundaries of any house of the horoscope (and sometimes more than one does so) will distinguish the particular conditions under which the effects related to that house are obtained. They describe everything connected with that particular part of the horoscope. Then again, the positions in the various parts of the horoscope of the Sun, Moon and planets will also have their special interpretations; and, finally the whole pattern of the horoscope and the link-ups therein of some planets with others, in their respective signs and house will be the general context into which any particular sign-position, any particular planetary placing, must be fitted. Very little can be known by merely considering isolated factors in any horoscope, for so much has to be balanced against so much else.

If you bear well in mind that the signs of the zodiac, Sun, Moon and planets must function according to their natures, no matter what place they have in the nativity and no matter what they are linked up with therein, and if you also remember that they can be interpreted from a positive or passive point of view, that is to say, in connection with the attitude and actions of the person or the circumstances in which he or she finds himself placed by the conditions imposed on him, you will find it easier to grasp their meanings. For then what seems alien to character, personality, talents, inclinations will be explained purely in terms of circumstance.

Let us therefore make a quick resumé of signs, Sun, Moon and planets from a comprehensive point of view, which embraces both their abstract principles and their concrete correspondences.

Signs

Fire signs:
Aries, Leo and Sagittarius. All very vital. Linked with idealism, personal magnetism, and the instinct for control over circumstance, with activities and methods of working and living in accordance with these. Denoting the people who are the leaders, the organisers of the others. Exuberant in everything, whether it be dealing with money, occupations,

relationships. Linked, naturally, with the 1st, 5th and 9th houses; so that the things connected with all these will play a dominant part in their lives and circumstances.

Earth signs:

Taurus, Virgo and Capricorn. All of them symbols of what is materialistic, solid, consistent, enduring; and so linked with persistence, practicality, prudence, and with activities and methods of working and living. Denoting the people who help to sustain what the leaders, the organisers have initiated. Controlled in their actions and attitude, whatever or whoever they are dealing with.

These signs are correlated with the 2nd, 6th and 10th houses; so the things connected with all these will play a dominant part in their lives and circumstances.

Air signs:

Gemini, Libra and Aquarius. Symbolic of what is communicative, and therefore co-ordinative. Signs which are "Airy" and therefore symbols of intelligence as the vital force, and of people who function primarily on the plane of the mind rather than through their emotions, or else, as in the case of Libra, are able to attain equilibrium of mind and emotion discriminative in everything, whether it be money-matters, activities or adjustment to other people and to circumstances.

These signs being linked, naturally, with the 3rd, 7th and 11th houses, the things connected with them will play a dominant part in their lives and circumstances.

Water signs:

Cancer, Scorpio and Pisces. Connected with sensation, emotion, with sensitivity, intuition, receptivity, assimilation; passive (with the exception of Scorpio) in action, but powerful nonetheless. Signs linked with the enigmatic processes of the life and death cycle, and therefore very complex in nature. Denoting the people who, through their emotional attitude, and emotional impact on others, ensure the continuance of the phenomenon of the life as we know it.

These signs are naturally linked with the 4th, the 8th and the 12th houses, and the things connected with them will play a dominant part in their lives and circumstances.

All these details about the elemental groups and their sign-correspondences and house-correspondences will provide you with the clues to their life-histories in general.

But further clues will be given by the relative positions in the horoscope of the Sun, Moon and planets; which, again are to be interpreted in accordance with their basic principles.

Sun

The sun is the symbol of the ego, the real self of the individual; and also of his vital force. Whichever sign of the zodiac is occupied by the sun, and whatever house of the horoscope is occupied by the Sun and its sign, will be the most important focal-point in the horoscope-pattern.

Say we find the Sun in Scorpio and in the fourth house. Here we have a person activated by tremendous emotional force, striving for emotional security and focussing his or her vitality on things concerned with the home, family. This person will be happiest and most successful when operating from the home-base; the type of activities carried on will in some way be connected with, or conducted from, the home, or through the family, or perhaps be the result of family influence. Whatever else is active in the horoscope pattern will in some way or other make its way into the domestic pattern.

But, and this is also most important, we must bear in mind that as particular focus has thus been stressed upon the fourth house of this individual's horoscope, special concentration must also be turned upon the sign that is the natural ruler of that house (in this case, Cancer) and the position it occupies in the horoscope, the effects of any planets which may be in that sign in the horoscope, and also the position of the Moon, ruler of Cancer, which with Mars, ruler of Scorpio, the occupier of the 4th house, will all have a very important bearing upon the individual's life.

This may sound terribly complex; in fact however, one more often than not finds that interpretations are underlined by making comparisons of this kind. This blending of sign and planetary "influence" has a connective effect which may be obvious or subtle, but it is still unmistakably traceable.

Moon

Whereas the Sun is the symbol of the ego, the Moon, in character-analysis, expresses the way in which the person reflects their environment, through their emotional reactions to it. You will see the link-up of the Moon with any sign in the expression of the individual's personality.

How, then, will this work out say, in the case of a person born at sunrise, with the sun-sign on the Ascendant (the part of the horoscope concerned with

114

personality as distinct from character)? Well, of course, if they happen to be born at New Moon, the Moon will also be in the first house and in the sun-sign; so character and personality will, as it were, be indistinguishable, being one and the same. Otherwise, the position and sign occupied by the Moon in that horoscope will make the personality function differently to that of its real nature when it is conditioned by certain circumstances, the circumstances applying to the sign and house occupied by the Moon.

As the Moon is the symbol of flux (the waxing and waning of the Moon is the reason that lies behind this analogy) so its position in a sign and in a house of the horoscope will indicate fluctuating conditions, a recurrent ebb and flow as it were, of the things, the relationships, the activities connected with that house and sign.

Mercury

Mercury is the planet connected with intelligence, with the flexible use of intelligence when it is exercised either creatively or discriminatively; and Mercury, being also linked with Gemini, a third-house sign, has to do with travel — minor travel; in other words, limited communications.

Whichever sign and house is occupied by Mercury in a horoscope will give an indication of the way in which the person's mind works, what their mental interests are focussed upon, the way in which their mental attitude is affected by whatever is connected with the house and sign; it will also show everyday contacts effected by the normal travel-routine of the person.

Should it be placed in the tenth house (career;

status) it means that the person will probably follow an occupation which is predominantly intellectual, which involves a good deal of variety as regards surroundings, contacts to do with the career; and it also suggests that the career-pattern will be a restless one, involving either numerous changes of job, or rather unstable prospects. If it occupies one of the earthy, stable signs, it will more probably mean continual variety of experience and environment but a steady job, all the same, for it will be "tethered" to some extent by its sign. It will then further particularise the actual type of Mercurial work performed in accordance with the nature of the sign.

Venus

Venus is a feminine planet, the symbol of peace, love, unity with the environment; but it is also connected with the Arts, entertainment, with everything that is pleasurable to the physical, rather than the mental, requirements. With Mars, it links up with the sensual aspect of a person's nature.

Its position, by sign and house, in the horoscope pinpoints the direction in which the person's happiness will be focussed. Further light on the significance of Venus would then be thrown by studying where Gemini, and Mercury, are placed in the horoscope and discovering the means by which a link-up between them and the position of Venus occurs.

Mars

Mars is the symbol of combative instincts, of sheer physical energy; of the sex-impulse (in a woman's horoscope it will show her emotional and physical reactions to men; in a man's horoscope it will relate to his sexual capacity, but his emotional and physical reactions to women will be seen through the position of Venus in the chart). Where questions of virility or fertility are concerned, the positions of both Venus and Mars must be carefully considered, according to the sex of the person.

The position of Mars in a horoscope will denote the sources from which tension, conflict occur, the factors that arouse, or demand, a combative reaction on the part of the person. If Mars is in the first house, the individual will be the cause of their own tensions by reason of their temperament. If in the sixth house it will link up with conditions of health, and relationships with co-workers.

Jupiter

Jupiter is the symbol of expansion; it is the planet linked with success, good luck. Its natural association is with Sagittarius and the 9th house, in particular, and thus mentally it denotes a mind which has a wide range of scope, an attitude of mind which embraces a philosophical, religious, humane outlook on life. It also has a strong link-up with Pisces, sharing rulership of this sign with Neptune. Perhaps rulership is a rather too definite term for this link-up of Neptune and Pisces, as it may be that the planet cannot definitely be so powerful in this connection — astrologers are not yet sure of this. Personally, I have found that the characteristics of Neptune accord more with Pisces than those of Jupiter.

The sign and house-position of Jupiter in a horoscope will denote the source from which fortunate experiences can be derived, benefits extracted in one way or another; it shows where the person has most scope to expand himself.

Thus, if in the 2nd (money) house, it suggests that the individual will be able to make money plentifully, and that in financial transactions luck tends to be on his side. It can also mean extravagant tendencies, but extravagance can only be indulged in when there is money around or in prospect.

In the 10th house it is a particularly good augury of success and distinction in career, and of an elevated status in life, according to the environmental background of the individual. In the 7th house it would denote fortunate, expansive partnerships; and so on.

Saturn

In contrast to Jupiter. Saturn has to do with the principle of limitation, frustration, rigidity – and frigidity. It is the planet which is the symbol of old age, with all its accompanying inconveniences.

So the sign and house-position of Saturn will indicate difficulties, disappointments in connection with the matters or circumstances involved; as it is the symbol of weight, it can also mean heavy responsibilities which cramp the individual. Again, it can relate to the impact of the influence of very much older people, especially those in the family, upon the individual and his circumstances. If connected with health, then it means illnesses that are chronic ailments, or ones from which it is difficult to recuperate; or, in the 6th house, it might merely mean close association with elderly, ailing people.

Uranus

Though one of the more recently discovered planets, the nature of Uranus has most clearly been defined. It is linked with electricity, and all that this implies. It has a galvanic form of self-expression, which can be constructive or destructive, but which is always very powerful, very positive, very abrupt. Thus it symbolises the element of surprise in experience; and, when linked with the mentality, indicates originality and a rebellion against all that is orthodox.

So, whichever sign it is in and wherever it is to be found in a horoscope there will be sources of sudden changes, unexpected events, opportunities, complications. In 5 th, 7th or 11th has a very positive effect on personal relationships, bringing them into being and dissolving them rapidly, highlighting them with very colourful associations.

Neptune

Neptune is linked with everything that is intangible, amorphous, misty and mysterious. It is connected with the intuitive, the mystic qualities inherent in the soul of Man; it also has to do with artistic creativity in a particularly refined form; but, because it is also connected with dissolution, it can be most disintegrative in its expression, no matter what it is connected with in the horoscope. Its sign and house-position will indicate what is most involved, unreliable, deceptive — or again what is most sublime, idyllic and "out-of-this-world". But it can never represent actuality; that is to say, there will either be something incomprehensible, something elusive, something over-intricate about its associations.

Pluto

No hard and fast interpretations are possible regarding the principle zone of particular influence in the zodiac or the exact nature of Pluto. All that can so far be deduced by tentative research over the past thirty odd years is that Pluto seems to be linked with the processes of dissolution and regeneration. It seems to function through the bringing to light of things which are obscure; the transformation of things through their dissolution and re-organisation; it is linked up in some way with all that we know of atomic fission, and the potentialities brought into being by the birth of the Atomic Age. Wherever it is placed in a horoscope it seems safe to assume that very marked, fundamental changes will transpire, whether they be in connection with character, career, relationships or activities.

In addition to their particular attributes, the planets have to be considered in connection (a) with their natural rulerships in the horoscope; that is, the places in the chart they are linked with because of their sign rulership; as for instance, Venus has a strong connection both with the 2nd (money) house and with the 7th (partnership house) because it is ruler of both Taurus and Libra. When, irrespective of its sign, a planet is found in its own house its significance will be more powerful and more harmonious. Then (b) there are the planetary relationships with signs other than their own, signs in which they are said to be "exalted" (or very powerful); signs in which they function weakly, and are in "detriment" because these signs are the opposite ones to those ruled by the planets; and the signs in which they are said to be in their "Fall" which not only weakens but can also add a perverted, or distorted quality to their attributes. Actually, these very ancient distinctions of planetary effects must be taken with some measure of caution, as, from personal experience I have not found that they are too reliable.

The link-ups are as follows; —

SUN: *exalted* in Aries; in its fall in te opposite sign Libra; (the Exaltation-Fall positions are always those of opposite signs). In its *detriment* in Aquarius, because this sign is the opposite to that of the sign ruled by the Sun — Leo.

MOON: *exalted* in Taurus; in its fall in Scorpio. In *detriment* when in its opposite sign, Capricorn.

MERCURY: *exalted* in Virgo (one of the signs it rules, by the way; it is distinctive from the other planets in this detail). In its *fall* in Pisces, and in *detriment* in both Sagittarius and Pisces, the signs opposite the "Mercurial" ones of Gemini and Virgo.

VENUS; *exalted* in Pisces; in its *fall* in Virgo. In *detriment* in the signs which are opposite the "Venusian" ones, i.e., Aries and Scorpio.

MARS: *exalted* in Capricorn; in its *fall* in Cancer; and in *detriment* in the two signs opposite to martial Aries and Scorpio, Libra and Taurus.

JUPITER: *exalted* in Cancer; in its *fall* in Capricorn; and in *detriment* in Gemini and Virgo, the signs opposite to the Jupiterian ones Sagittarius and Pisces.

SATURN: *exalted* in Libra; in its *fall* in Aries; and in *detriment* in Cancer and Leo, the signs opposite to the two which have a link-up with Saturn, Capricorn and Aquarius.

No particular distinctions can be made for Uranus, Neptune and Pluto; none of the signs which have been suggested by various astrologers can be considered as being too reliable in this respect.

5: HOW TO CALCULATE A HOROSCOPE

BEFORE going on to calculate a horoscope, let us assimilate some rudimentary astronomical facts, because it is better to understand why, as well as what, you are doing. Too many astrologers draw up their charts automatically, and this stunts their powers of interpretation.

The horoscope, as you know, is merely a diagrammatic representation of the positions occupied by the Sun, Moon and planets in the zodiac at any specific time selected, as observed from any particular part of the earth. So it represents a purely geocentric aspect of the heavens.

To an observer on the earth, it appears that the Sun, Moon and planets move in a great arc across a certain portion of the sky occupied by a sprawling belt of constellations, seemingly "fixed"; but that planets and constellations recurrently rise in the eastern sky, reach the Meridian and set in the west — to re-appear over the eastern horizon after an interval of time. But the observer is suffering from an optical illusion. In reality, it is the earth which — in moving round the Sun — gives this impression.

What is really happening is that the earth is orbiting the sun, carrying along with it its satellite the Moon (which is simultaneously circling the earth); and the planets, likewise, are also revolving around the sun, at different speeds and varying distances from each other. Two of the planets, Mercury and Venus, are nearer the sun than the earth; the rest lie beyond the earth. Of them, Mars is nearest our planet, and next to Mars is Jupiter; then come, in turn, Saturn, Uranus,

Neptune and — on the utmost fringe of the Solar System — Pluto.

The belt of constellations through which the planets seem to move, and which itself also rotates across the sky, is that of the *Zodiac*, with its twelve star-groups of different width and numbers of stars. The circumference of the whole belt is 360°.

The Zodiac extends approximately 8° above and below the plane of the ecliptic (which is the track the earth follows round the sun). The planets always keep within the limits of the 8° area, but they do not always remain exactly on the same plane as the earth; and their positions vertically above or below that plane are known as their latitudes north or south. It is from their latitudes and their longitudes (which are the distances they cover when apparently travelling through the degrees of the Zodiac) that the calculations for a horoscope are made, whereby they can be located according to the place of observation, and its own longitudinal and latitudinal equivalent on the earth.

But now something more about the Zodiac. At the time it was measured (by Hipparchus, a Greek astronomer of the second century B.C.) the beginning of the astronomical year, the Vernal Equinox as it is called, occurred when the Sun, starting its journey northwards in the heavens, actually entered (or seemed to enter) the constellation Aries. So Hipparchus proceeded to divide the unequally spaced twelve constellations into areas of 30° each. But, in doing so and in revising an ancient Babylonian catalogue of visible stars, he made a startling discovery. The so called Fixed Stars of the constellations no longer occupied the positions they had done when the Babylonians made their calculations; true, they had not shifted considerably, but nonetheless they had moved. This phenomenon is known as the *Precession of the Equinoxes;* and, again it is the result of the earth's movement.

For the earth, because of its shape, does not remain upright as it spins. In addition to rotating on its axis, and orbiting the Sun, it also quivers, as a top does when in motion, leaning over slightly at the poles from side to side. This makes the circumpolar stars seem to circle, too; and the Pole Star gradually shifts from Polaris, to Aldemarin, thence to Deneb, on to Vega and after that, to Thuban, after which Polaris again occupies the north point in the heavens. (At present, Polaris is our Pole star, and it will continue to be so for some time yet).

The Pole stars take some 25,800 years to complete their circling; in the course of which, at, approximately every 2,150 years there is also a major shift of the position of our Sun at the time of the Vernal Equinox. For the Precessional movement also seems to make the sun retreat gradually through the constellations. At present, the Sun is no longer in 0° of the constellation Aries when Spring begins in the northern hemisphere, but is way back in the constellation Pisces; from whence it will retrogress into Aquarius within some few hundred years (nobody seems quite sure when).

But it would be highly inconvenient for mathematicians to have to repeatedly change the name of the space in the ecliptic which the sun appears to occupy around March 21st of each year. They are basing their calculations on a time-pattern, not on actual star-groupings.

This is why it is not incorrect to state that there are two zodiacs; one, of course — the one we use for

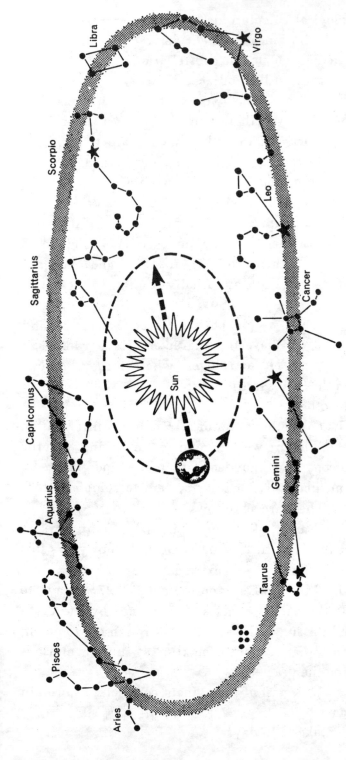

A diagram to show how the movement of the earth makes the Sun appear to move through the constellations.

125

astrological calculations, for instance – is a purely abstract time-measurement derived originally from the actual zodiac of constellations; but although abstract it is still a zodiac.

We are not sure when, how or why the constellations were given their names; but most probably it was because of the phenomena which appeared regularly at the times of the year when the Sun reached different areas of the ecliptic. Our seasons are in accordance with this, not because the Sun appears to be in Aries, Cancer, Libra or Capricorn, but because the Sun is moving between 0° and 90° of the ecliptic, then from 91° to 180°, and on again from 181° to 270°, and finally from 271° back to 0° Aries.

Therefore, people born between March 21 and April 20 will have the characteristics attributed to them by the old astrologers whether they be born when the Sun is in the constellation Pisces, Aquarius or the others.

The only other item of astronomical information you need before we can get down to dealing with the horoscope is a knowledge of the periods taken by the members of the solar system to complete their orbits. These are as follows: –

The Earth takes, approximately, 365¼ days to orbit the Sun; in the course of each four years this fraction adds up to an extra day – Leap Year.

The Moon takes, approximately, 27½ days to circle the earth; and, as it is carried by the earth round the sun, will seem to go through the zodiac in just less than a month, making 13 such revolutions during the year.

Mercury, fleetest of the planets, completes its orbit in 88 days.

Venus takes 225 days.

Mars takes 1 year and 322 days.
Jupiter takes 11 years and 315 days.
Saturn takes 29 years and 167 days.
Uranus takes 84 years and 6 days.
Neptune 164 years and 288 days.
Pluto takes 247 years and 255 days.

The Horoscope

To begin with, before you can draw up a horoscope you must know the year, date of month, time of birth (as near as possible) and the place of birth of the person concerned; if you were doing the nativity of someone you have not seen, you would also need to know their sex.

The date and time of birth are necessary so that you may know which sign the Sun was in at the time, and which sign was on the Ascendant of the place of birth; and the place of birth also particularises which degree of the ecliptic would be rising (on the Ascendant).

Once you have got the full birth data the rest is comparatively easy; for you then only have to refer to an EPHEMERIS and a TABLE OF HOUSES. The Ephemeris is a reference book of tabulations of the movements of the Sun, Moon and planets for any year, and gives the longitudes and declinations of the Sun and planets for Noon Greenwich Mean Time for every day; extending its calculations, so far as the Moon is concerned, to include midnight positions. You can buy one very cheaply.

By using your Ephemeris you will be able to convert the *clock* birthtime to its equivalent *sidereal* time (star time). This is necessary because clocktime is measured by the Sun, and the solar day is four minutes longer in time than a sidereal day, the time it takes the star-groups to make one (apparent) complete revolution through the heavens.

If you are doing the horoscope of someone born at or near Greenwich, or in other words, born in the latitude 51° 32′ North you will be able to complete all your calculations from your Ephemeris; as the Ephemeris includes a "Table of Houses" for that Latitude, and also ones for latitudes 40° and 53° North (where such cities as New York and Liverpool — among many others — are located). But if you are doing the horoscope of someone born in a different latitude, then you will also need to refer to the Table of Houses for it; and there is a convenient compact series of these gathered together in one volume (Raphael's Tables of Houses).

So far your calculations are purely astronomical ones; but having made them, and thereby having found in which signs the Sun, Moon and planets are placed at the time of birth, and which degrees of the ecliptic will be "ascending" or "culminating" (passing over the Meridian) at the time, the astronomical part of your work has been completed.

Two different charts will enable me to give you examples of the significance of the particular geographical location of birth. One is conveniently related to a birth taking place in London (so the Ephemeris alone is all you will need) and the other for one which occurred in the town of Brookline, Massachusetts, U.S.A. (for which you will also have to refer to the book of "Tables of Houses").

The London horoscope is that of H. M. Queen Elizabeth II, born at 1.40 a.m. Greenwich Mean Time, on the 21st April 1926, in Bruton Street, just off Piccadilly.

The first step is to find the sidereal time of birth

so that the framework of the horoscope – its Houses – may be constructed.

Now look in your Ephemeris for the pages concerning 1926. On one page you will see there are a series of columns with various headings; they give, in turn, the date of the month, the day of the week, the Sidereal Time at Noon, Greenwich Mean Time, on that day; and the longitudes and declinations of the Sun and Moon at Noon (and, in the case of the Moon, at midnight). The Latitude of the Moon is also given; you will not need to refer to this. All these columns occupy the lower portion of the page; above them are other columns giving the Latitudes (again not important to you) and Declinations of Neptune, Uranus (which is called Herschel, after the name of its discoverer) Saturn, Jupiter and Mars. With the exception of Mars, the declinations are for alternate days, because Neptune, Uranus, Saturn and Jupiter are so much slower in movement.

The other page of the Ephemeris gives again a series of columns which indicate the day of the month and the longitudes on each day, of Neptune, Uranus, Saturn, Jupiter, Mars, Venus and Mercury. Above those columns are others giving the Latitudes and Declinations of Venus and Mercury for each Day. There are other columns, one which gives the Moon's Nodes (which also need not concern you, for their positions in the horoscope are a matter of study for more advanced students of astrology) a column which lists the "Mutual Aspects" (for the moment we will ignore these, but we must come back to the matter of Aspects later on) and a series of columns which give the "Lunar Aspects".

Now, to find the Sidereal Time for the birth, we must proceed as follow. Because birth took place soon after midnight we start with the Sidereal Time for the *previous* Noon. At Noon of April 20th Sidereal Time was 1 hour, 51 minutes, 16 seconds.

To the sidereal time at Noon we add the birthtime, which is as follows: 13 hours. 40 minutes (1.40 am. 21st).

Then, because of the difference between clock-time and Sidereal Time, we must make a further calculation, allowing an extra 10 seconds of time for each clock-hour, and a fraction for the minutes of clock time, to bring it into alignment with the sidereal time of birth. This 10 second adjustment, for 13 hours and 40 minutes, amounts to 2 minutes and (approximately) 18 seconds of time.

We have now got

	H.	M.	S.
Sid. Time previous Noon	1.	51.	16.
Time elapsed to birth			
Time (or Time-Interval			
Elapsed)	13.	40.	0.
Acceleration on Clock-Time		2.	18.
Sidereal time at birth	15h.	33m.	34s.

Turning to the back pages of our 1926 Ephemeris, we shall find the Tables of Houses for London, spread over two pages. They give the degrees of the zodiac which will be rising, culminating, and on the "Cusps" (beginnings) of each house of the Horoscope for approximately four-minute intervals of Sidereal Time throughout the whole twenty-four hours of the Sidereal Day.

We have to look up the entry in the left-hand column, headed Sidereal Time, which approximates most closely to the Sidereal Time of birth. We find it in the right-hand page, on the upper portion of the page; it is 15h. 42m. 57s. Next to it, under the Zodiac symbols, are the degrees of the signs which will be over the 10th House (Meridian) the 11th House, 12th Houses; Ascendant (Rising sign) 2nd House and 3rd House.

Either boy or draw a horoscope-form, and insert the signs in the appropriate places.

You will notice that I have also inserted the remaining signs, which are of course, those opposite the six listed in the Tables of Houses, and which must be placed on the Cusps of 4th, 5th, 6th, 7th, 8th, and 9th houses, so that they follow the natural sequence of zodiac-signs. The degrees on these houses will be the same as those listed in the Tables of Houses.

One thing will probably strike you as being very curious about this framework of signs. In Houses 1 and 2, and in 7 and 8 a sign has been inserted (the technical term is "Intercepted"). No indication of that sign was given in the Table of Houses; you had to put it in, otherwise you would not have been able to complete the zodiacal circle, which must of course be in the natural order of the signs.

This brings up a matter which is the cause of much dispute among astrologers; and that is "House-Division". The Tables of Houses found in Ephemerides and in the familiar books which include a detailed list of them have been compiled according to the *Placidus* System of House division. But there are in fact six different systems of House division, and theories regarding other possible ones. The controversy over this problem of House Division — which centres upon which degrees of the zodiac should be related to the Cusps of the "intermediary"

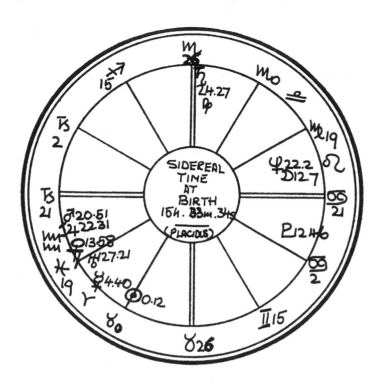

houses — and the trigonometrical methods by which they shall be computed — is much too complicated to be dealt with in the book. The Placidus House System has been selected for the purpose of the horoscopes included here because it is the one you are going to have to use when you come to buy yourself Ephemerides and Tables of Houses.

No matter what system of House division is used, the degrees on the Ascendant and the Meridian — the two key-points of a Horoscope will always be the same; and that is the really vital point.

When using the Placidus Table of Houses (or some others of the six Systems available) you will always have to be on the look-out for these "intercepted signs". They are explained by the fact that some signs of the Zodiac take a longer time so reach the horizon, either in the Northern or Southern hemispheres, than others.

In the northern hemisphere, the signs which take longest to rise are Leo, Virgo, Libra, Scorpio, Sagittarius and Capricorn; so Aquarius, Pisces, Aries, Taurus and Gemini become signs of "short Ascension". (In the Southern hemisphere the order is reversed.)

Having completed the outer framework of your horoscope, you now have to insert into it the Sun, Moon and planets, in accordance with the positions in longitude held by them at the time of birth.

So you turn back to the pages of the Ephemeris which list the longitudes for the Noon times of each day in April.

On April 20th they were as follows:
Longitude of Sun at Noon 29° 51′ 0″ Aries (♈)
Longitude of Moon Midnight 20th/21st (remember, the Moon Longitude is given for both Noon and Midnight, to make calculations easier, as it moves so much more swiftly than the rest) 11° 17′ 59″ Leo (♌)
Longitude of Mercury at Noon 4° 21′ Aries (♈)
Longitude of Venus at Noon 13° 24′ Pisces (♓)
Longitude of Mars at Noon 20° 28′ Aquarius (♒)
Longitude of Jupiter at Noon 22° 26′ Aquarius (♒)
Longitude of Saturn at Noon 24° 29′ Scorpio (♏)
Longitude of Uranus at Noon 27° 20′ Pisces (♓)
Longitude of Neptune at Noon 22° 2′ Leo (♌)

The planet Pluto was not discovered until 1930; all Ephemerides up to 1939 do not include its positions. But there is a book which gives them for the previous years. (This, and all other astrological books you might need at any time can be obtained from a London bookseller who specialises in this type of Literature; his name and address are given at the end of this book.)

Pluto's position on the 20th April 1926 was 12° 46′ Cancer (♋).

The Noon-time longitudes have to be adjusted to the actual Greenwich Mean Time of birth. In all horoscopes, the Sun, Moon and planet positions must always be inserted for Greenwich Mean Time.

It is very easy to make your calculations for the Sun, Moon and planets. All you need to be sure of, at this early stage in your studies, is that you have got the right degree; the minutes and seconds don't matter to you (they do, of course, to more advanced astrologers, engaged in very intricate interpretations which demand as great a degree of accuracy in calculation as is possible). But, in any case, it is only the Sun's and Moon's longitudes which are listed to seconds in the Ephemeris; the planets are only listed according to degrees and minutes of longitudes.

If you remember the rate at which the planets move through their orbits in a year you can soon gauge their daily revolutions. Mercury, of course, can move must faster than the others—though its 88 day revolution is erratic, because in some years it will continually be "retrograding". It is the most erratic of all the Sun's little family.

On average, Venus moves about 1° 12′ per day; Mars less than 1°, and the others (Jupiter, Saturn, Uranus, Neptune and Pluto, also much less than a degree. Allowing for the fact that there are sixty minutes to one degree, this amounts to five minutes of longitude to every two hours of clock time.

In the case of the Sun, this same rate of calculation applies; for it also only moves just a little under or over one degree of longitude in 24 hours; it can be 58 minutes to 1 degree 1 minute, no more or less.

The Moon, however, moves from anything between twelve to fifteen degrees of longitude in 24 hours; but as the Moon's Longitude is given both at midnight and Noon your calculations have to cover only half the day. Again, this can be done in your head, or on paper, without referring to logs.

Having already noted the noontime positions of the Sun, Moon and planets on the 20th, let us compare them with those of the 21st, and make the necessary quick calculations to bring them to the birthtime – 1.40 am. on the 21st).

Sun
Noon 21st; 0° 37′ 32″ Taurus (♉)
Noon 20th; 29° 39′ 0″ Aries (♈)
_____
Difference: 58′ 32″
Ergo: at 1.40 am. 21st the Sun will be approximately at 0° 12′ 18″ Taurus. (But 0° will serve for your purpose).

Moon
Noon 21st; 17° 12′ 16″ Leo (♌)
Midnight 20th/21st; 11° 17′ 59″ Leo (♌)
_____
Difference: 5° 54′ 17″
Ergo: at 1.40 am. on the 21st the Moon will be approximately 12° 7′ Leo. (12° will do for your purpose).

Mercury
Noon 21st; 4° 55′ Aries (♈)
Noon 20th; 4° 21′ Aries (♈)
_____
Difference: 0° 34′
(At 1.40 am = 4° 40′ Aries)

Venus
Noon 21st; 14° 23′ Pisces (♓)
Noon 20th; 13° 24′ Pisces
___

Difference: 0° 59′
(Note; Venus is moving rather more slowly than its average rate). (At 1.40 am. = 13° 58′ Pisces)

Mars
Noon 21st; 21° 11′ Aquarius (♒)
Noon 20th; 20° 28′ Aquarius
___

Difference: 0° 43′
(At 1.40 am. = 20° 51′ Aquarius)

Jupiter
Noon 21st; 22° 35′ Aquarius (♒)
Noon 20th; 22° 26′ Aquarius
___

Difference: 0° 9′
(At 1.40 am. = 22° 31′ Aquarius)

Saturn
Noon 21st; 24° 25′ Scorpio (♏)
Noon 20th; 24° 29′ Scorpio
___

Difference: 4′
(At. 1.40 am. = 24° 27′ Scorpio)

But note here that the planet has not moved forward, but backward; in the Ephemeris this is indicated by the figure ℞ which you will find near the top of Saturn's column. This so-called backward movement of the planets, Retrogradation, is not an actual fact but an illusion, and is caused by the earth's movement in relation to the planet.

Astrologers used to assume that a planet, when retrograde, had an unfortunate influence; personal experience does not bear this out, but rather that, when prediction is involved, the event will be retarded in time.

Uranus

Noon 21st; 27° 23′ Pisces (♓)

Noon 21st; 27° 20′ Pisces

Difference: 3′

(At 1.40 am. = 27° 21′ Pisces)

Neptune

Noon 21st; 22° 2′ Leo (♌)

Noon 20th; 22° 2′

Difference: −

Note: Neptune is also retrograde, but for the moment, stationary (At 1.40 am. = 22° 2′ Leo).

Pluto, like Neptune, is still in the same position — 12° 46′ Cancer (♋).

Declinations are equally easy to calculate; but as a beginner, it is best for you to ignore these; though they are given great importance by experienced astrologers.

Having located the Solar System's time-pattern at 1.40 am. you now have to insert it into the horoscope.

This is where you have to be particularly careful; for you might too easily put the planets in the wrong houses.

Bear in mind that the signs of the zodiac are inserted into the horoscope in an anti-clockwise sequence; and this also applies to the positioning of the planets.

If, as in the case of the present horoscope, Scorpio 25° is on the Meridian, and Saturn is in Scorpio 24°, then it must be inserted close to the cusp of the 10th house, but still actually just in the 9th House.

In the horoscope we are doing, Taurus 0° happens to be on the cusp of the 3rd house; and the Sun, being also in Taurus 0°, will be exactly on the cusp of that house.

Having completed the Queen's horoscope, let us now calculate that of the late President John Kennedy, who was born at 3 pm. Eastern Standard Time, on May 29th 1917, in Brookline, Massachusetts, U.S.A. The Latitude of birth was 42° 19′ N; and the Longitude 71° 6′ W.

Because all Ephemerides are calculated for G.M.T. we have to convert the Eastern Standard Time of 3 pm. into G.M.T. The difference between this particular Standard Time and that of Greenwich is five hours; and the birthplace being West of Greenwich this means it is 5 hours slow on G.M.T. So the equivalent to 3 pm. E.S.T. is now 8 pm. G.M.T.

We now have the information necessary to calculate the positions of the Sun, Moon and planets, but it does not serve any purpose for arriving at the sidereal (star-time) of birth necessary for calculating the Ascendant and Meridian degrees of the zodiac at the time of birth.

We must now pay special attention to the longitude of the birthplace — 71° 6′ West. We have to change this into *time*. Quite easy, because all we have to do is multiply by four (one degree of longitude is the equivalent of four minutes of time; one minute of longitude is four seconds of Time). So Longitude 71° 6′ W equals 4 hours, 44 minutes and 24 seconds of time (but we need not bother with the seconds; if they amounted to more than 30 one would be justifield in calling it 4 h, 45 m. of time).

Having found the equivalent of longitude in time, this must then be beducted from G.M.T. in order to find the local (not the Eastern Standard) time of birth.

Why? Because Standard Times, which are arrived

at by dividing the globe into 24 different Time zones, cover a whole 15° of longitude. They are official times used for convenience in synchronising clocks, but they do not tell us the true time, according to the star-positions. Once one has made the calculation from Standard to Greenwich Time, however, it is quite child's-play to find the true local time of birth; all that you have to do is to subtract (when the place is West of Greenwich) the longitude-in-Time from the G.M.T. If the place is East, you add it.

G.M.T. in this case being 8 pm. and the longitude-in-Time of Brookline being 4h. 44 minutes, the true local time will be 3.16 pm.

Therefore to your Sidereal Time for Greenwich at Noon you add 3h. 16 minutes, as follows;—

S. T. Noon	4 h.	25 m.	46 s.
Add	3 h.	16 m.	0 s.

and, to this, add Acceleration-
Interval of 10 secs. per hour   32.

Sid. Time at birth	7 h.	42 m.	18 s.

All we have to do now is to refer the Sidereal Time of birth to the latitude of the birthplace (42° 19′ N.) We need the Tables of Houses for this.

The nearest equivalent, at Latitude 42° North for the Sidereal Time at birth (7h.42.18s) is 7h.43m.34s. The house-cusps for the Horoscope, according to this, will be as follows;—

    10th — 24° Cancer
    11th — 28° Leo
    12th — 27° Virgo
    Ascendant — 20° Libra
    2nd — 17° Scorpio
    3rd — 19° Saggitarius

(no inconvenient "intercepted" signs to cope with here).

We can now fill in the sign positions in the President's Horoscope.

As for the positions of Sun, Moon and planets, reverting back to the Ephemeris we find, for G.M.T. Noon of May 29th 1917, and Noon of the 30th are as follows; —

Sun: *29th* – 7° 21′ 26″ Gemini (Ⅱ)
            30th – 8° 28′ 57″ Gemini

Moon: *29th* Noon – 13° 12′ 32″ Virgo (♍)
            29th Midnight – 19° 12′ 24″ Virgo

Mercury: *29th* – 20° 35′ Taurus (♉)
            30th – 20° 38′ Taurus

Venus: *29th* – 16° 21′ Gemini (Ⅱ)
            30th – 17° 35′ Gemini

Mars: *29th* – 18° 12′ Taurus (♉)
            30th – 18° 56′ Taurus

Jupiter: *29th* – 22° 59′ Taurus (♉)
            30th – 23° 13′ Taurus

Saturn: *29th* – 28° 8′ Cancer (♋)
            30th – 27° 14′ Cancer

Uranus: *29th* – 23° 43′ retrograde Aquarius (♒)
            30th – same position

Neptune: *29th* – 2° 40′ Leo (♌)
            30th – 2° 42′ Leo

Pluto: *29th* – 3° 14′ Cancer (♋)
            30th – same position

The birthtime of the President being 8 pm. G. M. T. you will have no difficulty in calculating the longitudes for that time; it is simply a question of dividing the times elapsed in each case by 3. (8 hours is one-third of 24 hours.) All you then have to do is insert them in your horoscope-chart. You can see the result on the facing page.

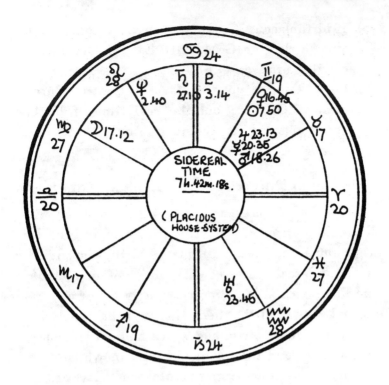

One last word on calculating horoscopes.

(1) The essentials for this are; —
Date and time of birth
Place of birth

(2) House-cusps are always calculated for Local Time (which of course may be the same as Greenwich Mean Time, according to the place of birth)

(3) Sun, Moon and planetary positions are always calculated for G.M.T.

(4) House-cusps are found by referring to the local sidereal time, arrived at by conversion of longitude of birthplace into Time and adjustment of this to Sidereal Time at Greenwich and, finally referring this back to the Latitude of the birthplace and the relevant Table of Houses.

(5) If birthplace is West of Greenwich, Local Time will be slow on G.M.T. If East of Greenwich it will be fast on G.M.T.

(6) Local Time is not Standard or Central European or G.M.T.; but the real time of birth, once converted into Sidereal Time.

Calculating Horoscopes for Southern Latitudes

Tables of Houses are only calculated for the Northern Latitudes. When you have to do a horoscope for a Southern Latitude of birth, you arrive at the Sidereal Time of birth by merely making one final calculation. Proceed exactly as for a Northern Latitude birth, then when you have got the Sidereal Time of birth, add on 12 hours. (This may take you beyond the 24 hour limit; in which case you deduct 24 hours from the total you arrive at.)

You then turn to the Table of Houses for the *degree* of Latitude that you want, find the exact or nearest-equivalent Sidereal Time that you want but, when it comes to writing in the signs you reverse them. If say, the Sidereal Time gives Gemini for the 10th House cusp, you put Sagittarius there; if the Ascendant is Leo, you put Aquarius. *No adjustment, of course, has to be made to the degrees listed.*

Finally, if you are in any doubt as to whether you have arrived at the right calculations, sit down and think things out. If you are calculating a horoscope for sunrise, the Sun (and its sign) must be on the Eastern horizon; if for Noon, it must be over the 10th house; if for sunset, then it will be on the 7th house. Other periods of the day will find the sun, in its sign somewhere between these points and the nadir, and so on.

6: INTERPRETING THE HOROSCOPE

HAVING learned how to construct a horoscope, you have now to interpret it; and it is at this point that astrology becomes completely divorced from astronomy.

Interpretation is based purely on symbolism and analogy; and, as such, is an art. But it is an art which is supported by an good deal of empirical evidence, a vast quantity of statistical data which is available to any serious student of astrology who cares to read and study the subject.

In order to be able to interpret a horoscope, you not only have to understand the meanings of the positions of the Sun, Moon and planets in the various houses and signs of the chart; but you also have to learn how to calculate and interpret the "Aspects".

Aspects are "angular relationships" established between the earth and planets. From a study of the pattern of aspects revealed by a horoscope it is possible to determine certain kinds of tensions which these angular relationships induce in the native. These aspects are measured in degrees, so that, for example, if the Sun is 180° from Saturn, then the luminary and the planet are in aspect. In this particular example, the two bodies are opposite each other in the horoscope, and the aspect is called "opposition".

The natal aspects are formed between bodies in the horoscope-pattern at the time of birth, due to their being at certain distances from each other in the zodiac at the time; at such positions they interreact, as it were, on each other, helpfully or otherwise, and this facilitates the interpretation of the horoscope in toto — it enables the student to make an intelligent synthesis of the whole thing.

The most important of the aspects are the CON-JUNCTION, SEXTILE, SQUARE, TRINE and OPPOSITION.

These are formed when the planets or luminaries are in the following angular relationships: (There are other, minor aspects, but these need not concern the beginner in astrology).

CONJUNCTION	0°	symbol	☌
SEXTILE	60°	symbol	✳
SQUARE	90°	symbol	☐
TRINE	120°	symbol	△
OPPOSITION	180°	symbol	☍

The sextile and trine aspects are harmonious in character; the conjunction is either harmonious, inharmonious or even ambivalent, according to which planets are involved in it; and the square and opposition aspects are inharmonious.

The harmony or disharmony is that much more accentuated when the "natures" of the planets are taken into consideration. Thus, a sextile or trine between Venus and Jupiter, and between the Sun or Moon and Venus or Jupiter, will be specially harmonious; a sextile or trine between Mars and Saturn is in itself good, but both planets are symbol of less congenial qualities than the other two.

A conjunction between the Sun and Moon, and the Sun or Moon and Mercury, Venus, or Jupiter is considered particularly harmonious; that between either of the luminaries and Mars, Saturn and Uranus must be considered inharmonious; that between Sun or Moon and Neptune is ambivalent.

The aspects between Sun, Moon and planets do not have to be absolutely exact in degree in the birth map; for an "orb" is allowed.

The orb is an allowance in degrees from the exact aspect, within which the significance of the relationship between the bodies is still considered to hold. For example, if Saturn is, say, 176° from the Sun, it is still considered to be in opposition.

In the case of a *conjunction*, it may be considered operable if, when the luminaries are involved, an orb of twelve degrees is allowed. Thus Sun or Moon will "conjunct" any planet when either is exactly in line with them, or up to twelve degrees away from them. If however it is the Sun and Moon which are jointly involved (meaning that the birth has occured near time of New Moon) then an orb of fifteen degrees is permissible. In the case of any aspect between the Sun, Moon and planets other than the conjunction (i.e., where it is a case of sextile, square, trine or opposition) a uniform orb of ten degrees should be allowed.

In cases where it is the planets themselves which form mutual aspects, the safe rule is as follows:

Sextile — allow up to 7 degrees orb
Square — allow up to 10 degrees orb
Trine — allow up to 10 degrees orb
Opposition — allow op to 10 degrees orb.

It must be admitted that astrologers do not entirely agree as to exactly how much orb must be allowed for each aspect. Clearly, the more precise the aspect is, the stronger the force exerted by the aspect will be, and this must be taken into account in an interpretation.

Aspects are not only formed by the planets at the time of birth, but they continue to be formed as the solar system revolves, and each planet completes its orbit. In this book we shall not be dealing with the "progressed" horoscope which concerns itself purely with the prediction of future events — the events foreshadowed in the birth-pattern being now exactly timed, by aspects formed by the moving planetary bodies, *both in relation to each and in relation to the positions they occupied at the time of the birth.*

These progressions are made at the rate one day for one year of birth. So, if you wanted to know what was likely to happen to someone whose horoscope you had calculated when they reached, say, the age of twenty-five years, you would count forward in the Ephemeris twenty-five days from the date of their birth.

Taking the positions of the Sun and planets at noon on that day, and readjusting these to conform to the hour the birth occurred, you would then look to see whether they formed any specific aspects with the birth-pattern. (As regards the mutual positions on that day, you would not have to take any trouble, as these are listed in the "Aspects" columns of each monthly section of the Ephemeris). Having noted down any particular aspects, you would then have a general indication of the overal prospects in store for the person concerned for the year following their 25th anniversary.

But, in order to time such prospects in more detail, you would then "progress" the Moon. This would mean studying its rate of movement between Noon of the 25th and 26th days (you will remember it can move between 12 and 15 degrees in a day); then bringing its position from Noon on the 25th day to that of the birthtime (say, for instance, 6 pm.) and then progressing it at the rate of anything from one degree to one-degree-and-a-quarter over the following twelve months. After which you go through the now familiar process of finding whether during its year's progress it has formed any aspects with the Sun, Moon or planets at birth, and also noting what aspects it has formed with the "progressed" planets on the 25th day after birth (these are also listed clearly in the Ephmeris to facilitate your job — it merely means making a mental calculation to see in which month the various listed aspects would fall).

All of this sounds more difficult than it really is; make a special effort, right from the time you start to calculate horoscopes, to do as many of your calculations without reference to logarithms, but by mental arithmetic. For your present purposes, all your calculations can be done this way, and it will help you to memorise the rates of planetary movements, to assess aszects much more quickly.

In the interpretation of progressed aspects you follow the same procedure as in analysing the significance of the planets, and their groupings, at birth.

Aspects to Mars will involve combative activity, successful or otherwise according to the nature of the aspect; aspects to Venus will indicate greater harmony and all the other things with which Venus is associated, and so on and so forth.

As to the extent of effect of any aspects, whether they be *Solar aspects* (those formed by the Sun to planets), *Mutual aspects* — those formed by the planets mong themselves — or *Lunar aspects* — their strength must be gauged by the positions in the birth-chart, and the aspects they formed, at birth. If, say, Jupiter is near the Meridian at birth, any aspect of Jupiter (inharmonious as well as harmonious) will have some benefit, and offer extended opportunities to "rise" in the world; but if Jupiter has inharmonious aspects from the Sun, Moon or planets at birth, then even the most powerfully beneficent progressed Aspect cannot exert itself to its fullest extent, and an inharmonious one will have greater power than it would otherwise exercise.

By carefully studying a birth horoscope you can easily assess, even without any reference to your Ephemeris, when, approximately, major "aspects" will be formed. Allowing for the one-degree-for-a-day (and consequently for a year) method, it is quite obvious when the Sun will reach any particular aspect with planets in the chart.

Then, if you remember that it takes the Moon approximately twenty-eight years to move right round the horoscope, so that for approximately two and a half years it will be in any one sign, you can quite quickly gauge where it will be in a certain year, and what aspects it will form in the following year allowing for its 12° to 15° rate of movement.

You will not of course take into consideration the more complicated details of progression, which involve the angles (the cardinal points of the chart) and the Sun, Moon and planets. For one thing, you have to be absolutely certain of birth-time in order to be able to make such calculations, and experienced astrologers spend a great deal of time working this out by careful research into events.

What you will be doing is to gain a sufficiently accurate judgment of the birth-pattern and potentialities of the person concerned to be able to gain a great deal of insight into their characters and lives.

Now let us get on with the actual business of interpretation. I have drawn up twelve different horoscopes for you to study, taking a different zodiac type in each case; so you have twelve case-histories which illustrate the way in which the sun-sign will function when part of a complex pattern formed at any particular moment in time. They are the horoscopes of very famous people about whom you will probably know a lot already; or, if not, can easily find out more through standard reference books, and this will help you to "dig deeper" into their character and life-histories.

Horoscope No. 1: Vincent van Gogh

Brief Case-history : Dutch Post-Impressionist painter, son of Calvinist pastor. Artistic family connections; uncle a picture-dealer (van Gogh started off at 16 by working in his firm); cousin also a painter (from whom van Gogh took some lessons). Family connections also very powerful in another way; throughout his life, van Gogh was protected by his brother, whose faith in his art remained unshaken, and who helped him whenever possible. Had a chequered career; at one time was a teacher of languages in Ramsgate, also worked among the Belgian miners. This was because he had a strong religious impulse, wanted to enter the Church, and studied theology. Eventually ended up in Paris, where, in the artistic colony, he joined with other painters in the new techniques and developed his own style. Obssessed with a passion for vivid, barbaric. colours, and his technique was unscientific, spontaneous, exotic, fierce. Became friends with Gaugin. Always of a highly sensitive, nervous disposition, van Gogh began to show acute mental disturbance — partly aggravated by earlier privations in Belgium and excessive exposure to the hot sun of Southern France. After threatening Gaugin in a

SIDEREAL TIME 23.30.59

Name: Vincent van Gogh
Born: 10.38 am GMT 30 March 1853
Place: Groot Zundert, Holland
Lat: 51°15′N   *Long:* 5°30′E

150

moment of frenzy with a knife, he cut off his own ear in remorse. From February 1889 onward his mind was overcast by the shadow of insanity, and eventually he shot himself and died on July 29, 1890, at the early age of 37.

Synthesis of Horoscope-Pattern

A very clear reflection of his personality, work and life-history. Note 10th house position of Sun and Mercury in Fiery Aries, both in trine to Moon in Fiery Sagittarius; Moon being conjunct Jupiter (in its own sign) in 6th. Moon is ruler of Ascendant Sign, Watery Cancer; Mars, ruler of sun-sign, is in Watery Pisces, very close to Midheaven degree, and conjunct Venus. Neptune, also in Pisces, squares Moon. Mercury squares both Ascendant sign and degree; sun is ruler of third house.

Predominant focus of planetary activity is on 6th and 10th houses (work, health, career).

Thus, the character would be tempestous, combative, but complex due to the intense emotional sensitivity, receptivity to sensation (Cancer rising, Mars conjunct Venus in Pisces, quadrating Moon and Jupiter). Water signs are very closely linked with Painting, also with religious instincts (together with Fire signs; bear in mind that Moon and Jupiter are in Sagittarius, itself the sign of the Church). Idealism and altruistic instincts are the result of the blend of Fire and Water signs. Posthumous fame, after neglect during his life-time, indicated by the link-up of planets in Fire sign, combating the square of Moon and Jupiter to natal Mars, and of Moon to Neptune. Overtaxing of physical system by work, deprivation, also indicated by the 5th-house positions; particular emphasis of sunlight on state of mind indicated by Sun being ruler of 3rd house (intellect). General highly-strung mental-emotional attitude emphasised by Water signs (Cancer always noted for Moodiness; and note Moon in 6th). Love of vivid colours, which undoubtedly provided a release for pent-up emotions, indicated again by Water/Fire blending in chart-pattern.

Tragic end to life foreshadowed by Mars in wide conjunction with Sun (and in sign of self-destruction, Pisces); abrupt end to life by Saturn/Uranus conjunction (rulers of 8th house — manner of death). Strong family influence on life, and protection afforded by brother, result of Cancer (family sign rising) lunar conjunction with protective Jupiter; and Sun, (ruler of 3rd houses — brothers).

Horoscope No. 2: Dr. Sigmund Freud

Brief Case-History: Founder of psycholanalysis; and most frequently associated, in the layman's mind, with sex and its psychological signifiance. Had no instinctive interest in Medicine, but wanted to do scientific research. But, influenced by Goethe's essay on Nature, entered into medical training, starting with botany and chemistry. Worked in physiological and anatomical laboratories, decided to relinquish research work, owing to financial pressure, and take up neurology. Became interested in hypnosis, which formed the starting-point of his career in psychoanalysis. Much attacked by medical colleagues, but continued to study clinical psychology. Turned from technique of hypnosis to that of "association of ideas" in order to track down causes of psychological disturbance; made very important discoveries in connection with this, and especially that of the importance of the unconscious. Worked alone for ten years at psychoanalysis; but was then

Radio Times Hulton

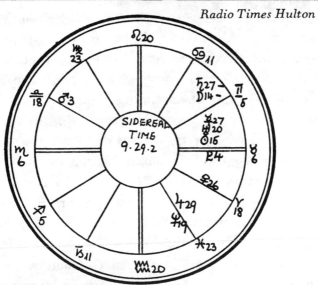

Name: Sigmund Freud
Born: 5.36.44 pm GMT 6 May 1856
Place: Freiberg, Germany
Lat: 50°56′N Long: 13°19′E

153

joined by several colleagues, among them Professor Jung. Personal life-history seems to have been unsatisfactory in connection with marriage (for details, refer to various biographies). Worked up to the end of his long life, dying in London September 23rd, 1939, just after outbreak of World War II. (Had fled from Germany as a result of the Nazi regime).

Synthesis of Horoscope-Pattern

Very typical of the tenacity, but somewhat restricted attitude, of those born with prominent fixed-sign groupings. Satellitium in a fixed sign (sun-sign, Taurus, in 7th house); a fixed Water-sign, Scorpio (sign to do with sex, and with delving into the origins of things), ascending. Venus, ruler of sun-sign, in a Mars sign, Aries, in 6th house (work; Sun ruler of 10th house, Career). Mars, ruler of ascending sign, in Libra; both Venus and Mars in their signs.

Choice of career very easy to establish; Leo (Medical sign) on Midheaven; Venus, ruler of sun-sign, in 6th house (health matters as a medium for occupation). Also indicates a very good physical constitution. Mars, ruler of ascending sign, in highly discriminative sign Libra; and Scorpio rising, indicative of preoccupation with the mysteries of the mind, and with the sex-force in its action on character and personality (Scorpio). Note, too, Moon and Saturn in 8th house (penetration into origins). And, incidentally, Saturn in good aspect to Venus — death through old age — natural causes.

Enforced as well as desired collaboration with others in carrying out of work indicated by emphasis of planetary activity in 7th house — partnerships, or group-activities. Difficult relationships with close professional colleagues, attacks from medical opp-

Mansell Collection

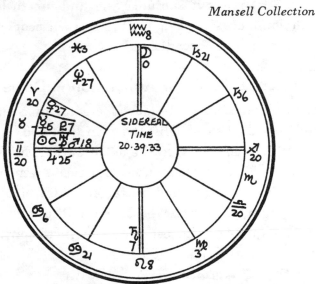

SIDEREAL
TIME
20.39.33

Name: Sir Arthur Conan Doyle
Born: 4.55 am GMT 22 May 1859
Place: Edinburgh, Scotland
Lat: 55°55′N *Long:* 3°10′W

onents, and marital problems also indicated by emphasis of activity on 7th, position of Uranus therein and of Pluto close to cusp of this house. Reason for preoccupation, first with hypnosis, then with dreams, can be accounted for by fact that Moon is ruler of 9th house (the "higher" mind – i.e., the inspirational faculties, dream-consciousness) in aspect to nebulous Neptune; Sun also aspects Neptune.

Freud has been criticised as being too one-pointed in his medical theories; this is to be expected of anyone with planetary emphasis in Taurus and Scorpio, which are fixed signs.

One last and interesting indication of enforced uprooting from native land, and death abroad; Saturn and Uranus are co-rulers of 4th (home, family, homeland); Saturn conjuncts Moon (enforced travel abroad Moon is ruler of 9th house – travel abroad); Uranus is conjunct Sun and in 7th house (7th house usually prominent in cases of people who travel or reside abroad).

Horoscope No. 3: Sir Arthur Conan Doyle

Brief Case-History: Immortal creator of Sherlock Holmes. English novelist, born in Scotland. Began career as a doctor; versatile as an author, his work included historical romances; but made famous by his detective stories and characters. Also became a playwright, and wrote books on military matters and war-propaganda; became a convinced spiritualist; died on July 7th, 1930.

Synthesis of Horoscope

Very typical of the Air groupings and of literary activities. Note satellitium in Sun-sign, Gemini, which is also on the Eastern horizon; in temperament Conan Doyle was typical of his sun-sign, intellectual and analytical.

Fame indicated by very exact trine of Sun and Moon; Moon — symbol of public favour — being just past the Meridian-point. Jupiter rising also emphasises personal prestige.

Note, too, 12th house position of Mercury in conjunction with Pluto; 12th house has to do with mysteries; here is evidence of the mind delving into them, and expressing its fascination for detection through a literary medium.

Versatility of talents again indicated by strong emphasis on Gemini; early links with medicine, and its influence on his work, accounted for by Saturn in Leo, in good aspect (sextile to Sun); Scorpio, one of the medical signs, intercepted in 6th house. Change of career, however, very typical of Gemini, which is prone to this course of action, or to diffusing career-activities.

Conan Doyle's conversion to spiritualism is not so easily accounted for; there is no very pronounced emphasis on Water signs (usually linked with intuition, preoccupation with so-called "occult" matters); but bearing in mind emphasis on the 12th house (what lies behind or beneath the surface of things) and allowing for the close sextile of Neptune with both Moon and Sun, the riddle is solved. Undoubtedly led to an interest in Spiritualism through friends — note Neptune's 11th house position in Water-sign, Pisces.

The award of a title accounted for by the prominence of Jupiter as well as by solar-lunar trine.

Longevity assured by good aspect of Sun to Saturn, ruler of 8th house (manner of death). Venus, ruler of 6th, health, in good aspect (sextile) to Jupiter;

157

sound constitution; but preoccupation with other people's health at some time — i.e., medical work — (Venus in 12th).

Horoscope No. 4: The Duke of Windsor

Brief Case-History: Very romantic, and so universally-well known it hardly needs repetition. Idolised as the Prince of Wales; much devoted to his mother, the late Queen Mary; renounced his throne for the sake of love and loyalty to his sweetheart; forced into exile by Parliamentary decree. A would-be champion of the under-privileged — the miners.

Synthesis of Horoscope-Pattern

In this chart, it is the character which is especially interesting study; for the Duke did the blankly unexpected — in uniting himself with a Commoner, a foreigner; in marrying late; in abdicating from his exalted position in society. The romantic, idealistic, highly emotional Sun-Sign Cancer, the prominence of the Moon, its ruler, in another Water sign, Pisces; the position of Venus in its own Fixed/Earth sign, Taurus, in the third house (mind influenced by strength of emotions) all indicate the sensitive, highly emotional temperament of the Duke. But it is the enigmatic, galvanic Aquarius which is rising in the chart, and the aspects of Uranus, part-ruler of this sign, to both the luminaries, which indicated the instinct to rebel against convention, to go against the tide of pressures put on him by external circumstances, to do the unexpected at a time of crisis. The consequences of this are also shown by the fact that Jupiter, ruler of 10th house sign (Sagittarius), in the 4th house, in Detriment, conjunct both Neptune and Pluto — symbols of dissolution of secure

158

foundations, loss of powerful influence, status. Note, too, the strong "pull" of Uranus, from the 9th house (travel, residence abroad) to both luminaries – drawing him away from his country of birth.

Strong link with mother and sister are indicated by Venus in the 3rd house.

Troubles through romance and marriage? Look to the 5th and 7th houses, or rather their rulers. Mercury rules 5th house; and the sign on that house is Gemini, the traditional ruler of the U.S.A. Mercury is itself in the 6th house (one's subordinates or "inferiors" in rank, though more usually associated, in this connection, with employees rather than personal associates). For a man, anything affecting his emotional life must also be accounted for by lunar aspects, and Venusian aspects; in this chart Moon is in aspect to Uranus (complications in connection with women); Venus is in square to Ascendant sign and degree (Aquarius). It also forms mildly inharmonious aspects (which you need not bother with) with Mars and Sun.

Sun and Mercury are co-rulers of marriage house; Sun aspects Uranus, but harmoniously (here, instead of the possible interpretation of divorce after marriage, we have marriage with a divorcee – and a divorce from abroad – Uranus in 9th). Mercury, co-ruler of 7th, is in square to Saturn, delays-frustrations – in connection with marriage; material loss thereby – obvious consequence of relinquishing of kingship.

This is but a sketchy interpretation of the main features of interest in the horoscope; the Duke's background is so well known that one can trace out the other features of his personality and life-pattern which are in clear conformity with his horoscope.

Cecil Beaton

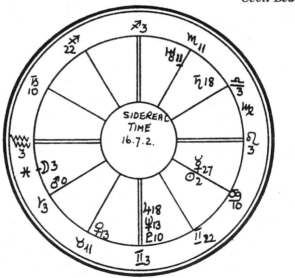

SIDEREAL TIME 16.7.2.

Name: Duke of Windsor
Born: 10 pm GMT 23 June 1894
Place: Richmond, England
Lat: 51°27'N *Long:* 0°0'' 18 W

Horoscope No. 5: Mata Hari

Brief Case-History: The woman-spy who was executed by the French in World-War I. Of obscure Dutch origins; married a Scotsman and went out to the Dutch East Indies with him. Marriage broke up; became notorous as a femme fatale, and held court in Paris; where she gave exhibitions to selected, distinguished audiences of "oriental dancing" — apparently her dancing did not amount to anything much, but her exotic personality and exhibitionist instinct carried the day. Today, there is some controversy as to whether she actually was a spy or merely an indiscreet and over-romantic female; apparently the riddle will not be solved because the French authorities refuse to make public the full records of the case against her. Faced the firing squad in 1917, at dawn on the 15th October, refusing to be blindfolded, and thanked the officer who was to give the command to fire. She was then 41 years old.

Synthesis of Horoscope-Pattern

This has a very flamboyant but tragic element about it. Satellitium in Leo accounts for her magnetic personality, reinforced by the dynamic Water sign which is rising, Scorpio; satellitium in Leo and Jupiter in Scorpio would also give her an exaggerated ego, the "folie de grandeur" illusion. Passionate emotional nature also indicated by this combination of Fire and Fixed-Water; especially as Mars, ruler of Ascendant sign, is in close conjunction with Sun in Leo.

Note the Moon-Saturn conjunction in a 12th house sign but in the 4th house. Accounts for comparatively lowly origins, and also for ultimate

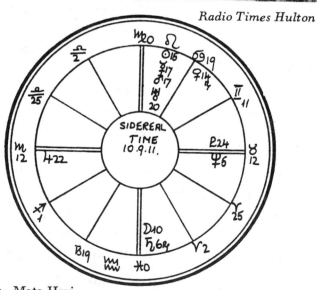

Name: Mata Hari
Born: 0.40.28 pm GMT 7 August 1876
Place: Leeuwarden, Holland
Lat: 53°15′N Long: 5°48′E

downfall; both are in square to the degree and sign on the 8th house — manner of death.

For details of her career, note in particular the square of Sun and Neptune; the fact that an 8th house sign (Scorpio — secrets) rises in the chart; the fact that Mars, ruler of both Acendant sign and 5th house (romantic attachments) is conjunct both Sun and Uranus, and also conjunct Mercury, ruler of 8th and 10th houses). This could account for betraying secrets imparted to her by men with whom she formed liaisons; it would account for the tragedy which brought her life to a close.

Mata Hari deliberately deceived the world at large by pretending that she was of oriental origin; the fascination which the Far East held for her is accounted for by the satellitium in the 9th house (distant travel; the living in a world of self-constructed fantasy).

Though, as a beginner of Astrology you cannot be expected to know this, even the sign associated with the 9th house (Cancer) the position of the Moon, its ruler (Pisces) and the location of the major satellitium in the chart in the south hemisphere of the chart would all account for her link-up with the Dutch East Indies. Ruler of her 7th house (marriage-partner) is Venus, which is in the Sign which rules Scotland (Cancer).

Horoscope No. 6:
Johann Wolfgang von Goethe

Case History: That of another great romantic, the most distinguished German poet; born in very good circumstances. Goethe was an eldest son; of several other children, only a sister survived infancy. She was one year younger than her brother. Goethe took after his mother in his personality and artistic gifts, but a certain strength of character came to him from his austere father; his nature was therefore balanced by the force of character acting upon a naturally warm-hearted, impulsive disposition.

Goethe himself recorded fully the details of his birth, and his horoscope; explaining how the proximity of Saturn to the Ascendant degree threatened his survival at birth.

Disillusionment over a very early love affair turned his interest to studious matters; he showed literary ability early on, and turned to poetry. He also studied Art. But he had a sudden haemorrhage, and was seriously ill for a long while. During the recuperative process, he became very introspective; he began to be interested in occult philosophy, and in astrology. He also turned to religious mysticism. Apart from his literary and art studies, he had also begun training for the law; and he resumed this on his recovery, and extended his interest to medicine.

His love-affairs were numerous, and his outpourings in verse and letters regarding these are prolific. In this he was typically Virgo, which loves to analyse and agonise over romance; one suspects, however, that mind dominated emotion in the final analysis. (Note the strong position of that rising Saturn in Scorpio, in sextile to Sun in a rational sign, Virgo).

A detailed analysis of Goethe's case history would take up far too much space; there is plenty of autobiographical as well as biographical data for interested students do draw upon.

Suffice it to add that he practised as an advocate, travelled a lot over the Continent, became attached to the German court at Weimar, continued to have

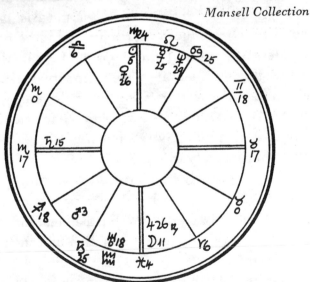

Name: Johann von Goethe
Born: Noon local time 28 August 1749
Place: Frankfurt
Lat: 50°7'N *Long:* 8°41'E

165

a succession of love-affairs, one of which drove him almost to the point of suicide; produced increasingly good poetry, came under the influence of distinguished men of letters as well as highly sophisticated people of the Court; legally married in his late fifties, but still maintained a roving eye. His varied literary output grew steadily in volume and distinction; and he is of course most famous for his composition of Faust. He died on March 22, 1832, at the age of 82, having established his supremacy as a lyric poet. His was a many-sided character, a crowded, vivid life; and, though predominantly an intellectual, he was also essentially a warm-hearted, impulsive, highly sensitive and idealistic human being.

Synthesis of Horoscope-Pattern

Once again, a very clearcut indication of the type of man and type of life-history. Earth and Water are strongly blended by the Sun sign and Rising Sun; but Fire is introduced very actively by the position of Mercury, ruler of Sun-sign, in Leo, in the 9th house (higher mental powers, spiritual faculties, inclinations) where it is joined by Neptune in the Water sign Cancer, in sextile to Venus in Earthy Virgo. Artistic creativity — not usual in Virgo, but here unmistakably evident.

The introspective element in his nature which preoccupied him with the deeper aspects of life, of love, are of course attributes of the blending of this Fire, Earth and Water combination and their locations in the chart.

Note the placing of Moon/Jupiter in 4th house; indicative of what Goethe inherited emotionally from his mother; of his comfortable family background. Saturn in the chart is clearly indicative, too, of the father's influence on his character, with its restraining qualities on an otherwise too restless nature (the Sun and Saturn, in astrology, are symbols of the male parent, and here they are in sextile in key-angles of the map).

The haemorrhage, and a tendency to nervous ailments, or to ailments brought on by over-strain on the physical system, are indicated again by the Venus position in Virgo (sun-sign; Venus being ruler of 6th house — health) in opposition to Jupiter — excess. But again, tenure of life would be strong, thanks to elevated position of Sun and Venus and solar aspect to Saturn; Saturn itself also being in sextile to the vitalising planet Mars (in a Saturn-sign, Capricorn). The very acute nervous stresses from which the poet suffered at times, mainly through his emotional entanglements, is denoted by the Mercury/Uranus opposition from 3rd to 9th houses.

A man of letters? Most certainly; for it is a Mercurial sign which controls the career-house; and, Mercury being in Leo, the dramatic fiery sign, what more natural than the works of Goethe should find their way into the Opera-House and the Theatre. (Incidentally, part of his skill for lyrical poetry would be accounted for by Scorpio rising, a naturally "musical" sign).

This horoscope is a field for very rich research and students are strongly recommend to read up fully the data available concerning Goethe.

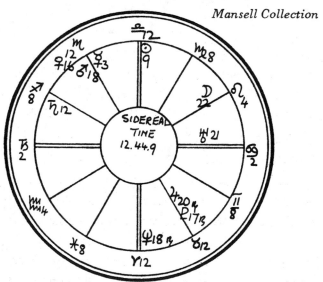

Name: Mahatma Gandhi
Born: 7.09 am GMT 2 October 1869
Place: Kathiawar, India
Lat: 18°45'N ·*Long:* 72°49'E

Horoscope No. 7: Mahatma Gandhi

Case-History: Again, so well known that it should be familiar to all readers of this little book. Famous Indian Nationalist leader; and a pacifist par excellence. A Hindu, born in good social circumstances; studied Law in London. Because he promised his mother he would eat no meat, nearly starved on the voyage over. Later became a vegetarian and very keenly interested in diet and personal hygiene. It helped him overcome his physical frailties and live to a very good age.

Had little confidence in himself as a lawyer, so had an unspectacular time in the early part of his legal career; but on going to practise Law in South Africa he was aroused by the plight of the Indians living there. He gave up his legal career, devoted himself to a very strict yoga-discipline.

Came into conflict with the South African government because of his activities, and suffered arrest and imprisonment, also physical assault, from Europeans and even from his own countrymen. He advocated farming as the most desirable means of existence; and always practising what he preached, became skilled in this and in the domestic arts, including nursing.

Gandhi's whole adult life-history was one of perpetual fighting for his ideals, and for home-rule for India; but his technique was a non-violent one. It is this, to which he held unswervingly, which most distinguishes him in political history. He was a fundamentally religious man; and a man of unimpeachable principles and unshakeable determination. He spent much time in meditation and prayer; lived an ascetic life, although he was a family man, too; he strove always to do good, and defeated his enemies by this instinct to return good for evil, to circumvent the forces of oppression. In temperament, he was most charitable and tolerant in spirit; but he was no tactful diplomatist and would always be honest about his opinions. He came to lead his country, but, alas, his policy of non-violence was too much to ask for less developed souls than his; and his life had a tragic end when, on January 30th 1958, whilst he was undergoing a voluntary fast as a protest against anti-Moslem riots, he was shot dead by a Hindu extremist, a member of his own religious group.

It has been written of him that though he had an ever-widening circle of friends, he had no intimate; for he never discriminated between them. To him, all men were brethren.

Synthesis of Horoscope-Pattern

Gandi's horoscope is an example of the power of the human spirit to reach sublime heights. None more truly lived the life of a saint, but a saint of practical dimensions, than this rather delicate man; who conquered his body and gave full rein to his soul. It is an example too, of the inexplicable something, the "X" factor in Man, that makes him not the slave, but the master of his destiny; for, it must be remembered, a number of people all over the world will have been born at times which gave them a birth-pattern approximating that of Gandhi, a birthdate shared with him, but only one such being was unique. It is the example of the man who controls and is not controlled by his stellar pattern. For a study of the chart shows numerous conflicts — conflict between will and desire, physical powers and moral stamina. It is the chart of a man who has very powerful emotions as well as a high-grade intellect and tremendous self-discipline; so that he must have suffered intense inner conflicts.

And it shows the best that is brought forth by the Air sign Libra in combination with the Earth sign Capricorn — signs not themselves in harmony by any means. But it is the Libran element which explains his policy of nonviolence, his love of humanity at large; and it is the Capricorn element that gave him the strength of will to carry out his purpose. Note the benefic sextile of Saturn, in a Fire sign (Sagittarius) to the Sun in its Air-sign, Libra.

His legal career, his prominence in public affairs are of course denoted by the position of Libra (one of the signs very common among those who follow the Law in any capicity); and this is underlined by Saturn in Sagittarius (another legal sign; but also one much concerned with religion and philosophy). The rigid discipline of yoga can be attributed to the 12th-house Saturn; the control of both conscious and unconscious forces within oneself. This same Saturn also explains his honourable imprisonment, indicating measures taken to control his activities.

The nature of his death is a little more obscure to interpret; but Venus, ruler of sun-sign is conjunct Mars in Scorpio (sign of death, and violent death at that); they are both in the 11th house, which means death through those who ought to be considered friends rather than enemies (fellow-Hindu assassin); the Moon in the 8th suggests a public death (he was out walking when it happened, and surrounded by people). Death, it may be added, is usually difficult to interpret in any horoscope, and this aspect of astrological interpretation should be left alone, except by those who are highly experienced and skilful professional astrologers who can be sure of all the difficulties attending such dangerous predictions.

The failure of Gandhi to perpetuate his system of non-violence during his life-time is due to the solar opposition to Neptune, which thwarts the full achievement of one's idealistic aims. This aspect, falling from Midheaven to Nadir points in the chart, also explains why, even though so much idolised, so greatly respected all over the world, the lesson he strove to teach has since been disregarded by humanity at large.

Horoscope No. 8: Pablo Picasso

Case-History: Very colourful, very tempestous. Painter, and the initiator of Cubism in modern painting. Son of an artist who was also Professor of Arts, and received his first lessons from his father. Settled in France in 1903. His techniques have changed from time to time, according to his various "periods"; he and Bracque jointly formulated the Cubist formula between 1906 and 1910. Unlike the impressionists, Picasso sought to create form — abstract form; which has been termed a "visual music". An extremely inventive painter, and a pioneer who blazed the trail for many followers; he has done designs for the stage.

His personal life has been vivid, and includes several lengthy liaisons; he is the father of several children; hates the idea of growing old, and remains an extraordinarily virile figure for a man now in his 85th year (1966). A recent autobiography written by the woman who shared his home for some years is particularly revealing as to his character.

Synthesis of Horoscope-Pattern

It is with Picasso the artist, rather than Picasso the

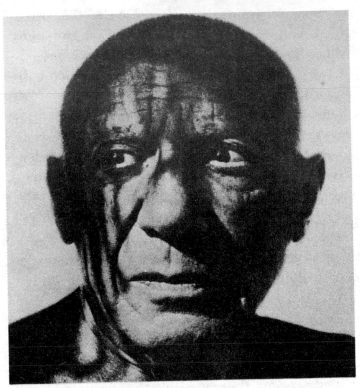

Horst Tappe

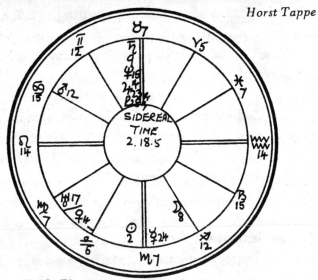

Name: Pablo Picasso
Born: 0.17.32 am GMT 25 October 1881
Place: Malaga, Spain
Lat: 36°43′N *Long:* 4°23′W

man, that we are dealing now. One of the Water signs (usually connected with Art) is his sun-sign; but the sign over the Meridian is an Earth one, albeit ruled by the artistic planet Venus, which is in its own other sign, Libra.

This would fully account for the desire for new *concrete* forms of art, the expression of the abstract in concrete terms — what seems to be a contradiction, in fact; but is only the natural result of the complexity of the Scorpio temperament seeking outlet through an artistic medium. Anything that Scorpio does to express itself will be in some way involved, yet very penetrating in that it "digs down to the roots" of things.

It is Mars, ruler of the sun-sign, which is the other indicator of his activity as an artist; for here it is in the Water sign Cancer — usually prominent in the charts of painters; it forms benefic aspects to the Sun, and to Saturn.

The association with Bracque, leading to the development of Cubism, is especially interesting when one bears in mind that Bracque was himself a Sun-Taurus.

As to the very full-blooded way in which Picasso has conducted his personal life, this is only to be expected of someone born with Sun in Fixed-Water Scorpio, Fiery Leo on the horizon, Mars in a strongly emotional and sensation-loving sign, Cancer; and Moon, ruler of Cancer, close to the cusp of 5th house (various romantic attachments).

Picasso is the father of several children — and the chart does indeed indicate the virility necessary for this.

Karsh of Ottawa

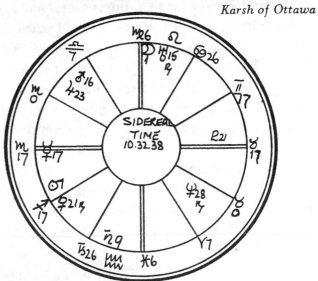

Name: Sir Winston Churchill
Born: 4 am GMT 30 November 1874
Place: Blenheim, England
Lat: 51°43'N   Long: 1°16'W

Horoscope No. 9: Sir Winston Churchill

Case-History: So well known that we will dispense with it altogether and plunge straight into the interpretation of the chart.

Synthesis of Horoscope-Pattern

Character and personality: the bonhomie, the ambition, the breadth of mind, vision, emotions natural to Sagittarius are here shown by Sun and Venus in that fiery sign; the strongly combative streak, the flair for witty, rapier-like repartee are denoted by the rising position of Mercury in Scorpio.

This is, indeed, a most vital horoscope; and one in which there is much that is fluid, so that the life-pattern would inevitably be eventful, changeful, right to the end.

Look at the trine aspect of Uranus to Sun (both in Fire signs) and the solar square with Moon; then, again, at the opposition aspect of Mercury and Pluto, both in square to Uranus; Uranus and Mercury being also inharmoniously aspected with Saturn. This would denote recurrent changes, successes alternating with failures, fluctuating popularity at some periods in life; but the Jupiter/Venus sextile, in which the planetary aspect is strengthened because each body is in the other's sign, would triumph in the end.

There is nothing small about anything in this chart; everything is on the grand scale, character, personality, associations, achievements.

A public career would be obvious, allowing for the position of the Moon just past Meridian point but the fact that he was a very undistinguished scholar in his youth (about which he often boasted) probably acounts for his preference for journalism in his early days. Mercury rising gave him his flair for writing, and Sagittarius is the orator's sign. Neptune in 5th house (education) opposing Mars (ruler of 5th) and Jupiter would account for lack distinction at school.

Venus in good aspect to Jupiter (Venus being ruler of 7th) explains his happy marriage; the position of Pluto in 7th would, in this case, affect public rather than private life, and would make for stresses in close links enforced on him by public activities.

Sir Winston's liking for painting as a relaxing hobby will be easily explained by Mercury in Water Scorpio (manual skill in a visual art).

Lastly, in actual physique the effects of the Sun-sign Sagittarius and the rising sign Scorpio are to be noted in the changes in appearance between the slim, handsome young man and the tough, bulldog thick-set appearance of the older Churchill; Sagittarius does put on weight in middle age, when it would especially show on a frame which is strong, sturdy (the Scorpio signature).

Horoscope No. 10: Cassius Clay

Case-History: Boxing Champion of the world. A negro and a recently converted Muslim; involved in political activities because of this. From what has been so widely publicised in the world-press about Cassius Clay, the reader will be familiar with his phenomenal boxing-history and the tremendous ballyhoo which has been built around him. But what of the real man? Let us now look at the chart to find out.

Synthesis of Horoscope-Pattern

This shows sun in Earthy Capricorn, the Air sign Libra rising; a satellitium in an Air sign, Aquarius (including the ruler of the Ascendant) in the 5th

Camera Press

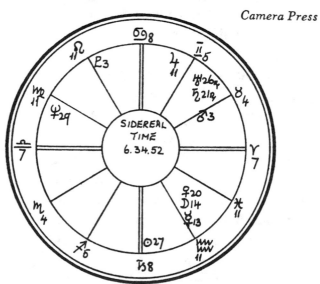

Name: Cassius Clay
Born: 4.30 am GMT (18th) 17 January 1942
Place: Louisville, Kentucky
Lat: 38°15′N *Long:* 85°45′W

house (entertainment); Uranus and Saturn in Taurus in the 8th house (ruled by Venus, which is in square to these planets) and Mars on the cusp of the 8th house, in square to the Sun. Jupiter is ruler of the 3rd house (mentality) and Jupiter is in the sign of its Detriment, Gemini, and in the 9th; but in harmonious aspect with the satellitium in Aquarius (including a trine to Mercury, ruler of 9th house). Neptune, in Earthy Virgo, is also harmoniously aspected (trine) with Sun and also with Uranus (Saturn being ruler of Sun-sign).

Uranus harmoniously aspect Capricornian Sun, emphasising the emportance of Earth-grouping in this chart.

The horoscope shows an intelligent mind, and a tendency to over-inflated vanity and exaggerated ambition (effects of Jupiter in Gemini). But, though combative, this is not an aggressive chart, so we can well believe that the bloodthirsty remarks made by Clay are merely publicity window-dressing. However, the solar square to Mars indicates a quick temper which could be physically violent when much provoked. There is an idealistic strain in the make-up which comes from the rising Libra, and aspects of Venus (in an Air sign, Aquarius – humanitarian sign) to Mercury, Moon and Jupiter. Cassius Clay's religious attitude will certainly be completely genuine; and there will be an idealistic attachment towards romance.

Moon, ruler of 10th well aspected with Venus and Jupiter would bring success in any public career; and, as the Moon is in the 5th house, together with the ruler of the Ascendant sign, it is clear that some form of public entertainment would be involved in the career. That this should be professional sport will be a matter of accident rather than design; for one would not unhesitatingly pick out sport as the obvious method of earning a living. Mars in good aspect with Meridian sign and degree would however mean succes in sport, once this was selected. (Incidentally, it is the Earthy signs which produce the greater number of sporting figures who concentrate on fisticuffs; but in view of the position of Mars near the cusp of the 8th and the positions of Saturn and Uranus, one hopes that Clay's boxing career will not be brought to an unfortunate conclusion through physical injury. He would do well to get out of the game whilst still very young and on top.

His tremendous speed, the lightness of his feet, are the natural attributes of Libra — a sign associated with harmonious movement, dancing; this also will give a very good sense of timing.

The less happy aspects of Cassius Clay's early home life have been so widely publicised that there is no harm in referring to them; they are shown by the solar square to Mars.

Horoscope No. 11: Lord Byron

Brief Case-History: Father, a libertine; mother, a foolish, passionate woman of violent temper, possibly mentally unbalanced; parents separated before the birth of their son. His mother was much attached to Byron, but not a good influence on him; spent most of her money on his welfare. Byron, who succumbed to infantile paralysis, was lame from birth; the right leg and foot were most affected. On the death of his great-uncle he gained the family estates and title; but did not enter upon his inheritance till ten years later (1808). Went to Cambridge in October 1805;

Mansell Collection

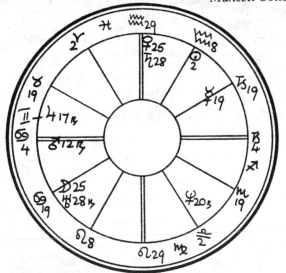

Name:　Lord Byron
Born:　2 pm GMT 22 January 1788
Place:　London
Lat:　51°32'N　*Long:* 0°

181

tooks his seat in the House of Lords in March 1809 and made his maiden speech in February 1812. His mother had died the previous year, and also three of his friends. Married in January 1815, a Taurean wife; the marriage broke up in January 1816; a daughter had been born on Dec. 10th 1815.

The scandal-mongering surrounding his relations with his half-sister was aired at this time, and Byron was forced to leave England. Byron's amours are a matter of history for, as he said, he was not blessed with the "gift of continency"; but they served their purpose as they fed his poetic genius; women contributed to his fame, in fact. Temperamentally, he was kind, generous, truthful, never spent beyond his means; romantic, temperate and courageous; but he could be self-indulgent, over-emotional. Of medium height and strong build, he had a pale skin, a very striking eye, and was described by a contemporary as "beautiful" — having a classical cast of features. He had to fight his tendency to put on weight.

His first poetry was published in 1816/17; *Childe Harold* appeared in March 1818; his greatest work — *Don-Juan* — was published in 1823/4. Whereupon, to quote his own words "I woke one morning to find myself famous."

Although he had no political influence in England, Byron enjoyed a great reputation as a champion of liberty abroad; notably among the Greeks. He had first visited the Balkans as early as 1809/10: he was in Greece, hoping to participate in the Greek Revolution, when he died from a chill contracted at Missolonghi. He died on April 19th 1824. It is doubtful whether he would have died so young but for the fact that a sound constitution had been undermined by his excesses in his thirties.

The unhappy circumstances of his childhood are shown by the Sun, ruler of 4th, opposition Uranus; break-up of the family. The mother's over-indulgence, financially, and her general influence on the son are also shown by the conjunction of Moon and Uranus in the Money house.

His lameness may be attributed to afflictions of Sun, Saturn and Uranus (i.e., Sun opposition Uranus; Moon conjunct Uranus; Saturn conjunct Venus — Saturn and Uranus are planets connected with paralysis; Uranus is here ruler of Sun-sign, and Saturn is co-ruler). Sagittarius, which rules the upper part of the leg, is in the 6th house; Aquarius, of course, rules the ankles.

His amours, and the scandal surrounding his relations with his half-sister, can be defined by the 5th house Neptune, in a Venus sign (Libra). Venus being conjunct Saturn, ruler of marriage-house, explains the unhappy ending to this relationship. Incidentally, to the end of his life Byron vainly hoped for a reconciliation with his wife. The break-up of this marriage separated him from his daughter, which he deeply regretted; another illegitimate child (also a daughter) died in the convent in which he had placed her. Like most men with Cancer rising, he had a strong sense of affection and duty towards his children. The fact that his amours contributed to his poetic inspiration is also shown by the elevated Venus, which, with Saturn, trines Neptune. It is curious how in this chart everything affecting relations with women are under curiously ambivalent influences: Moon conjunct Uranus; Venus conjunct Saturn; Moon and Uranus square Neptune; a feminine sign rising (Cancer). Women largely controlled the pattern of his life, though he seems to have found it difficult to enjoy much peace with most of them. His own "lack of continency" is of course due to the rising Mars in Cancer.

The Aquarian signature is however discernible in his preoccupation with the cause of Liberty; both in Italy and Greece he was much involved in this. The fact that he continually flouted convention was of course another facet of his Aquarian characteristics; and he was certainly extremely erratic and perverse in behaviour from time to time.

Horoscope No. 12: Albert Einstein

Brief Case-History: Famous Physicist; renowned for his Relativity Theory. Of Jewish parentage, and raised in comfortable surroundings. Professor Einstein taught mathematics and physics whilst taking his Ph. D., and published his first papers on physical subject at this time. In 1909 he was appointed extraordinary Professor of Theoretical Physics at the University of Zurich; and he took the Chair of Physics (in Prague) in 1911, returning as full Professor to his Zurich polytechnic school in 1912. In 1913, he became Director of the Kaiser-Wilhelm Physical Institute at Berlin.

By this time, his intellectual prestige had brought him a stipend to enable him to devote his full time and energies to research. He became a foreign member of the Royal Society, and in 1926 was awarded a gold medal by the Royal Astronomical Society in recognition of his Theory of Relativity, the preliminary work on which he had begun way back in 1905. He received a Nobel Prize in 1921.

He married twice, and his second wife died in 1936; he had two sons; and was an exile from Nazi Germany (like Freud.)

Synthesis of Horoscope-Pattern

I chose this chart as a sample of the Piscean horoscope because it shows the full possibilities of this curiously involved sign. In himself, Einstein was a most unworldly man, careless of his appearance, content with a very simple way of life, desiring no possessions, absent-minded — the traditional scientist. In his work he was a brilliant star that outshone all his contemporaries.

Many Pisceans possess good mathematical potentialities; in this map, these are emphasised by the 10th house position of Sun. But it is not this sun which is so significant from this point of view (though it indicates distinction in whatever career would be chosen); but rather the positions of Jupiter, and Moon. Jupiter is in the 9th house (higher thought; abstract thought; philosophical thought) but it is in a scientific sign (Aquarius), which would direct the interest into Science. Sagittarius, the sign ruled by Jupiter and the natural ruler of the 9th house, is on the cusp of the 6th (type of work engaged in) Moon is in that sign in trine of Venus (Moon being ruler of Ascendant house). Here the nature of the work can be traced, also the instinct to devote the whole of the energy to the working vocation (Einstein seems to have been uninterested in social life). Both Sagittarius and Aquarius are signs which indicate breadth of activities, constant progress; this would make for pioneer work of very wide implications. And, indeed, his Relativity Theory has caused a complete revolution in scientific thought; he is the Copernicus of the 20th century.

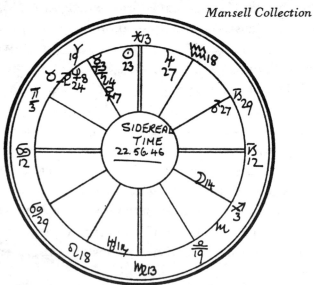

SIDEREAL
TIME
22.56.46

Name: Albert Einstein
Born: 10.50 am GMT 14 March 1879
Place: Ulm, Germany
Lat: 48°23'N *Long:* 10°E

Water signs are much concerned with Physics as well as Medicine; and of course with research work, especially that type of research which demands an inspirational, intuitional as well as totally rational approach. One wonders, therefore, if Einstein grasped his complicated theories intuitively before he set out to rationally explain them.

There is no very special emphasis on the personal side of life, apart from the fact that the "family" sign Cancer is rising; and Einstein was a family man. Mars in square to Venus could account for break-up of the first marriage; and Moon square to Sun would indicate unsatisfactory domestic links.

We have now completed the brief interpretations of the twelve representative horoscopes. As you will have noted, interpretation is not a simple, clearcut matter, but one demanding mental ingenuity; nothing is altogether obvious, some factors are rather obscure. But they are logical when one carefully reflects about the natures of the planets, their natural rulerships as well as their accidental positions in the birth-chart; and when too one remembers to link the signs and planets which are natural rulers of each section of the map with those signs and planets happening to occupy houses.

If astrological interpretation was a perfectly straightforward matter it would soon become tedious; as it is the more you examine charts the more you are able to glean from them; and each and every one presents something new for your consideration. Therein lies the fascination of astrology; it can never become a cut-and-dried technique. Dealing as it does with the intricacies of human nature and human behaviour it presents endless themes of interpretation.

Familiarise yourself with it by doing the horoscopes of all the people you really know intimately. If you come up against details which are bewildering, think and think again until you have hit upon the solution. With practice your deductive methods will refine themselves; increased confidence will enable you to extend your judgment.

Of course, if you decide to go into the subject deeply you will need to read some good textbooks to add to the rudimentary knowledge I have given you; and I have listed some which are well worth serious attention. But never take textbook interpretations too literally; they can never substitute for your own judgment.

Bibliography:

CARTER Charles E. O.,
   The Principles of Astrology. Theosophical Publishing House, 1925
DAVISON Ronald C.,
   Astrology. Arco Publications, 1963
GLEADOW Rupert S.,
   Astrology in Everyday Life. Faber and Faber, 1940
HONE Margaret E.,
   The Modern Text Book of Astrology. L. N. Fowler & Co., 1951
LEO Alan
   The Horoscope and How to Read it. L. N. Fowler & Co., 1902
LEO Alan
   The Key to Your Own Nativity. L. N. Fowler & Co., 1910
LIND Ingrid
   Astrology and Commonsense. Hodder & Stoughton Ltd., 1962
MAYO Jeff
   Teach Yourself Astrology. English Universities Press Ltd., 1964
ROBSON Vivian E.,
   A Student's Textbook of Astrology. Cecil Palmer, 1922
ROBSON Vivian E.,
   A Beginner's Guide to Practical Astrology. T. Werner Laurie, 1931
PAGAN Isabella M.,
   From Pioneer to Poet. Theosophical Publishing Society, 1911

MELVIN POWERS SELF-IMPROVEMENT LIBRARY

ASTROLOGY
__ ASTROLOGY: HOW TO CHART YOUR HOROSCOPE *Max Heindel*	5.00
__ ASTROLOGY AND SEXUAL ANALYSIS *Morris C. Goodman*	5.00
__ ASTROLOGY MADE EASY *Astarte*	5.00
__ ASTROLOGY, ROMANCE, YOU AND THE STARS *Anthony Norvell*	5.00
__ MY WORLD OF ASTROLOGY *Sydney Omarr*	7.00
__ THOUGHT DIAL *Sydney Omarr*	4.00
__ WHAT THE STARS REVEAL ABOUT THE MEN IN YOUR LIFE *Thelma White*	3.00

BRIDGE
__ BRIDGE BIDDING MADE EASY *Edwin B. Kantar*	10.00
__ BRIDGE CONVENTIONS *Edwin B. Kantar*	7.00
__ BRIDGE HUMOR *Edwin B. Kantar*	5.00
__ COMPETITIVE BIDDING IN MODERN BRIDGE *Edgar Kaplan*	7.00
__ DEFENSIVE BRIDGE PLAY COMPLETE *Edwin B. Kantar*	15.00
__ GAMESMAN BRIDGE—Play Better with Kantar *Edwin B. Kantar*	5.00
__ HOW TO IMPROVE YOUR BRIDGE *Alfred Sheinwold*	5.00
__ IMPROVING YOUR BIDDING SKILLS *Edwin B. Kantar*	4.00
__ INTRODUCTION TO DECLARER'S PLAY *Edwin B. Kantar*	5.00
__ INTRODUCTION TO DEFENDER'S PLAY *Edwin B. Kantar*	5.00
__ KANTAR FOR THE DEFENSE *Edwin B. Kantar*	7.00
__ KANTAR FOR THE DEFENSE VOLUME 2 *Edwin B. Kantar*	7.00
__ SHORT CUT TO WINNING BRIDGE *Alfred Sheinwold*	3.00
__ TEST YOUR BRIDGE PLAY *Edwin B. Kantar*	5.00
__ VOLUME 2—TEST YOUR BRIDGE PLAY *Edwin B. Kantar*	5.00
__ WINNING DECLARER PLAY *Dorothy Hayden Truscott*	5.00

BUSINESS, STUDY & REFERENCE
__ CONVERSATION MADE EASY *Elliot Russell*	4.00
__ EXAM SECRET *Dennis B. Jackson*	3.00
__ FIX-IT BOOK *Arthur Symons*	2.00
__ HOW TO DEVELOP A BETTER SPEAKING VOICE *M. Hellier*	4.00
__ HOW TO SELF-PUBLISH YOUR BOOK & MAKE IT A BEST SELLER *Melvin Powers*	10.00
__ INCREASE YOUR LEARNING POWER *Geoffrey A. Dudley*	3.00
__ PRACTICAL GUIDE TO BETTER CONCENTRATION *Melvin Powers*	3.00
__ PRACTICAL GUIDE TO PUBLIC SPEAKING *Maurice Forley*	5.00
__ 7 DAYS TO FASTER READING *William S. Schaill*	5.00
__ SONGWRITERS' RHYMING DICTIONARY *Jane Shaw Whitfield*	7.00
__ SPELLING MADE EASY *Lester D. Basch & Dr. Milton Finkelstein*	3.00
__ STUDENT'S GUIDE TO BETTER GRADES *J. A. Rickard*	3.00
__ TEST YOURSELF—Find Your Hidden Talent *Jack Shafer*	3.00
__ YOUR WILL & WHAT TO DO ABOUT IT *Attorney Samuel G. Kling*	5.00

CALLIGRAPHY
__ ADVANCED CALLIGRAPHY *Katherine Jeffares*	7.00
__ CALLIGRAPHER'S REFERENCE BOOK *Anne Leptich & Jacque Evans*	7.00
__ CALLIGRAPHY—The Art of Beautiful Writing *Katherine Jeffares*	7.00
__ CALLIGRAPHY FOR FUN & PROFIT *Anne Leptich & Jacque Evans*	7.00
__ CALLIGRAPHY MADE EASY *Tina Serafini*	7.00

CHESS & CHECKERS
__ BEGINNER'S GUIDE TO WINNING CHESS *Fred Reinfeld*	5.00
__ CHESS IN TEN EASY LESSONS *Larry Evans*	5.00
__ CHESS MADE EASY *Milton L. Hanauer*	3.00
__ CHESS PROBLEMS FOR BEGINNERS *edited by Fred Reinfeld*	5.00
__ CHESS SECRETS REVEALED *Fred Reinfeld*	2.00
__ CHESS TACTICS FOR BEGINNERS *edited by Fred Reinfeld*	5.00
__ CHESS THEORY & PRACTICE *Morry & Mitchell*	2.00
__ HOW TO WIN AT CHECKERS *Fred Reinfeld*	3.00
__ 1001 BRILLIANT WAYS TO CHECKMATE *Fred Reinfeld*	5.00
__ 1001 WINNING CHESS SACRIFICES & COMBINATIONS *Fred Reinfeld*	5.00

__ MAKING MONEY AT THE RACES *David Barr*	5.00
__ PAYDAY AT THE RACES *Les Conklin*	5.00
__ SMART HANDICAPPING MADE EASY *William Bauman*	5.00
__ SUCCESS AT THE HARNESS RACES *Barry Meadow*	5.00
__ WINNING AT THE HARNESS RACES—An Expert's Guide *Nick Cammarano*	5.00

HUMOR

__ HOW TO FLATTEN YOUR TUSH *Coach Marge Reardon*	2.00
__ HOW TO MAKE LOVE TO YOURSELF *Ron Stevens & Joy Grdnic*	3.00
__ JOKE TELLER'S HANDBOOK *Bob Orben*	5.00
__ JOKES FOR ALL OCCASIONS *Al Schock*	5.00
__ 2000 NEW LAUGHS FOR SPEAKERS *Bob Orben*	5.00
__ 2,500 JOKES TO START 'EM LAUGHING *Bob Orben*	5.00

HYPNOTISM

__ ADVANCED TECHNIQUES OF HYPNOSIS *Melvin Powers*	3.00
__ BRAINWASHING AND THE CULTS *Paul A. Verdier, Ph.D.*	3.00
__ CHILDBIRTH WITH HYPNOSIS *William S. Kroger, M.D.*	5.00
__ HOW TO SOLVE Your Sex Problems with Self-Hypnosis *Frank S. Caprio, M.D.*	5.00
__ HOW TO STOP SMOKING THRU SELF-HYPNOSIS *Leslie M. LeCron*	3.00
__ HOW TO USE AUTO-SUGGESTION EFFECTIVELY *John Duckworth*	3.00
__ HOW YOU CAN BOWL BETTER USING SELF-HYPNOSIS *Jack Heise*	4.00
__ HOW YOU CAN PLAY BETTER GOLF USING SELF-HYPNOSIS *Jack Heise*	3.00
__ HYPNOSIS AND SELF-HYPNOSIS *Bernard Hollander, M.D.*	5.00
__ HYPNOTISM *(Originally published in 1893) Carl Sextus*	5.00
__ HYPNOTISM & PSYCHIC PHENOMENA *Simeon Edmunds*	4.00
__ HYPNOTISM MADE EASY *Dr. Ralph Winn*	3.00
__ HYPNOTISM MADE PRACTICAL *Louis Orton*	5.00
__ HYPNOTISM REVEALED *Melvin Powers*	3.00
__ HYPNOTISM TODAY *Leslie LeCron and Jean Bordeaux, Ph.D.*	5.00
__ MODERN HYPNOSIS *Lesley Kuhn & Salvatore Russo, Ph.D.*	5.00
__ NEW CONCEPTS OF HYPNOSIS *Bernard C. Gindes, M.D.*	7.00
__ NEW SELF-HYPNOSIS *Paul Adams*	7.00
__ POST-HYPNOTIC INSTRUCTIONS—Suggestions for Therapy *Arnold Furst*	5.00
__ PRACTICAL GUIDE TO SELF-HYPNOSIS *Melvin Powers*	3.00
__ PRACTICAL HYPNOTISM *Philip Magonet, M.D.*	3.00
__ SECRETS OF HYPNOTISM *S. J. Van Pelt, M.D.*	5.00
__ SELF-HYPNOSIS A Conditioned-Response Technique *Laurence Sparks*	7.00
__ SELF-HYPNOSIS Its Theory, Technique & Application *Melvin Powers*	3.00
__ THERAPY THROUGH HYPNOSIS *edited by Raphael H. Rhodes*	5.00

JUDAICA

__ SERVICE OF THE HEART *Evelyn Garfiel, Ph.D.*	7.00
__ STORY OF ISRAEL IN COINS *Jean & Maurice Gould*	2.00
__ STORY OF ISRAEL IN STAMPS *Maxim & Gabriel Shamir*	1.00
__ TONGUE OF THE PROPHETS *Robert St. John*	7.00

JUST FOR WOMEN

__ COSMOPOLITAN'S GUIDE TO MARVELOUS MEN Fwd. by *Helen Gurley Brown*	3.00
__ COSMOPOLITAN'S HANG-UP HANDBOOK Foreword by *Helen Gurley Brown*	4.00
__ COSMOPOLITAN'S LOVE BOOK—A Guide to Ecstasy in Bed	7.00
__ COSMOPOLITAN'S NEW ETIQUETTE GUIDE Fwd. by *Helen Gurley Brown*	4.00
__ I AM A COMPLEAT WOMAN *Doris Hagopian & Karen O'Connor Sweeney*	3.00
__ JUST FOR WOMEN—A Guide to the Female Body *Richard E. Sand, M.D.*	5.00
__ NEW APPROACHES TO SEX IN MARRIAGE *John E. Eichenlaub, M.D.*	3.00
__ SEXUALLY ADEQUATE FEMALE *Frank S. Caprio, M.D.*	3.00
__ SEXUALLY FULFILLED WOMAN *Dr. Rachel Copelan*	5.00
__ YOUR FIRST YEAR OF MARRIAGE *Dr. Tom McGinnis*	3.00

MARRIAGE, SEX & PARENTHOOD

__ ABILITY TO LOVE *Dr. Allan Fromme*	7.00
__ GUIDE TO SUCCESSFUL MARRIAGE *Drs. Albert Ellis & Robert Harper*	7.00
__ HOW TO RAISE AN EMOTIONALLY HEALTHY, HAPPY CHILD *A. Ellis*	5.00

__ MAGIC OF THINKING BIG *Dr. David J. Schwartz*	3.00
__ MAGIC OF THINKING SUCCESS *Dr. David J. Schwartz*	7.00
__ MAGIC POWER OF YOUR MIND *Walter M. Germain*	7.00
__ MENTAL POWER THROUGH SLEEP SUGGESTION *Melvin Powers*	3.00
__ NEVER UNDERESTIMATE THE SELLING POWER OF A WOMAN *Dottie Walters*	7.00
__ NEW GUIDE TO RATIONAL LIVING *Albert Ellis, Ph.D. & R. Harper, Ph.D.*	7.00
__ PROJECT YOU *A Manual of Rational Assertiveness Training Paris & Casey*	6.00
__ PSYCHO-CYBERNETICS *Maxwell Maltz, M.D.*	5.00
__ PSYCHOLOGY OF HANDWRITING *Nadya Olyanova*	7.00
__ SALES CYBERNETICS *Brian Adams*	7.00
__ SCIENCE OF MIND IN DAILY LIVING *Dr. Donald Curtis*	5.00
__ SECRET OF SECRETS *U. S. Andersen*	7.00
__ SECRET POWER OF THE PYRAMIDS *U. S. Andersen*	7.00
__ SELF-THERAPY FOR THE STUTTERER *Malcolm Frazer*	3.00
__ SUCCESS-CYBERNETICS *U. S. Andersen*	6.00
__ 10 DAYS TO A GREAT NEW LIFE *William E. Edwards*	3.00
__ THINK AND GROW RICH *Napoleon Hill*	5.00
__ THINK YOUR WAY TO SUCCESS *Dr. Lew Losoncy*	5.00
__ THREE MAGIC WORDS *U. S. Andersen*	7.00
__ TREASURY OF COMFORT *edited by Rabbi Sidney Greenberg*	5.00
__ TREASURY OF THE ART OF LIVING *Sidney S. Greenberg*	5.00
__ WHAT YOUR HANDWRITING REVEALS *Albert E. Hughes*	3.00
__ YOUR SUBCONSCIOUS POWER *Charles M. Simmons*	7.00
__ YOUR THOUGHTS CAN CHANGE YOUR LIFE *Dr. Donald Curtis*	7.00

SPORTS

__ BICYCLING FOR FUN AND GOOD HEALTH *Kenneth E. Luther*	2.00
__ BILLIARDS—Pocket • Carom • Three Cushion *Clive Cottingham, Jr.*	5.00
__ CAMPING-OUT 101 Ideas & Activities *Bruno Knobel*	2.00
__ COMPLETE GUIDE TO FISHING *Vlad Evanoff*	2.00
__ HOW TO IMPROVE YOUR RACQUETBALL *Lubarsky Kaufman & Scagnetti*	5.00
__ HOW TO WIN AT POCKET BILLIARDS *Edward D. Knuchell*	5.00
__ JOY OF WALKING *Jack Scagnetti*	3.00
__ LEARNING & TEACHING SOCCER SKILLS *Eric Worthington*	3.00
__ MOTORCYCLING FOR BEGINNERS *I. G. Edmonds*	3.00
__ RACQUETBALL FOR WOMEN *Toni Hudson, Jack Scagnetti & Vince Rondone*	3.00
__ RACQUETBALL MADE EASY *Steve Lubarsky, Rod Delson & Jack Scagnetti*	5.00
__ SECRET OF BOWLING STRIKES *Dawson Taylor*	5.00
__ SECRET OF PERFECT PUTTING *Horton Smith & Dawson Taylor*	5.00
__ SOCCER—The Game & How to Play It *Gary Rosenthal*	5.00
__ STARTING SOCCER *Edward ꞏlan, Jr.*	3.00

TENNIS LOVERS' LIBRARY

__ BEGINNER'S GUIDE TO WINNING TENNIS *Helen Hull Jacobs*	2.00
__ HOW TO IMPROVE YOUR TENNIS—Style, Strategy & Analysis *C. Wilson*	2.00
__ PSYCH YOURSELF TO BETTER TENNIS *Dr. Walter A. Luszki*	2.00
__ TENNIS FOR BEGINNERS, *Dr. H. A. Murray*	2.00
__ TENNIS MADE EASY *Joel Brecheen*	4.00
__ WEEKEND TENNIS—How to Have Fun & Win at the Same Time *Bill Talbert*	3.00
__ WINNING WITH PERCENTAGE TENNIS—Smart Strategy *Jack Lowe*	2.00

WILSHIRE PET LIBRARY

__ DOG OBEDIENCE TRAINING *Gust Kessopulos*	5.00
__ DOG TRAINING MADE EASY & FUN *John W. Kellogg*	3.00
__ HOW TO BRING UP YOUR PET DOG *Kurt Unkelbach*	2.00
__ HOW TO RAISE & TRAIN YOUR PUPPY *Jeff Griffen*	5.00

*The books listed above can be obtained from your book dealer or directly from
Melvin Powers. When ordering, please remit $1.00 postage for the first book
and 50¢ for each additional book.*

Melvin Powers

12015 Sherman Road, No. Hollywood, California 91605